Peter Salz

Towards Patient-specific Electrical Impedance Tomography

Peter Salz

Towards Patient-specific Electrical Impedance Tomography

Using 3D Thorax Models

Südwestdeutscher Verlag für Hochschulschriften

Impressum / Imprint
Bibliografische Information der Deutschen Nationalbibliothek: Die Deutsche
Nationalbibliothek verzeichnet diese Publikation in der Deutschen Nationalbibliografie;
detaillierte bibliografische Daten sind im Internet über http://dnb.d-nb.de abrufbar.
Alle in diesem Buch genannten Marken und Produktnamen unterliegen warenzeichen-,
marken- oder patentrechtlichem Schutz bzw. sind Warenzeichen oder eingetragene
Warenzeichen der jeweiligen Inhaber. Die Wiedergabe von Marken, Produktnamen,
Gebrauchsnamen, Handelsnamen, Warenbezeichnungen u.s.w. in diesem Werk berechtigt
auch ohne besondere Kennzeichnung nicht zu der Annahme, dass solche Namen im Sinne
der Warenzeichen- und Markenschutzgesetzgebung als frei zu betrachten wären und
daher von jedermann benutzt werden dürften.

Bibliographic information published by the Deutsche Nationalbibliothek: The Deutsche
Nationalbibliothek lists this publication in the Deutsche Nationalbibliografie; detailed
bibliographic data are available in the Internet at http://dnb.d-nb.de.
Any brand names and product names mentioned in this book are subject to trademark,
brand or patent protection and are trademarks or registered trademarks of their respective
holders. The use of brand names, product names, common names, trade names, product
descriptions etc. even without a particular marking in this works is in no way to be
construed to mean that such names may be regarded as unrestricted in respect of
trademark and brand protection legislation and could thus be used by anyone.

Coverbild / Cover image: www.ingimage.com

Verlag / Publisher:
Südwestdeutscher Verlag für Hochschulschriften
ist ein Imprint der / is a trademark of
OmniScriptum GmbH & Co. KG
Heinrich-Böcking-Str. 6-8, 66121 Saarbrücken, Deutschland / Germany
Email: info@svh-verlag.de

Herstellung: siehe letzte Seite /
Printed at: see last page
ISBN: 978-3-8381-3961-6

Zugl. / Approved by: Kaiserslautern, TU, Dissertation, 2014

Copyright © 2014 OmniScriptum GmbH & Co. KG
Alle Rechte vorbehalten. / All rights reserved. Saarbrücken 2014

This dissertation is dedicated to all my friends and family who accompanied me through my life. Without their friendship, love and support, this work would not have been worth doing.

Acknowledgments

Many wonderful people have contributed in some way or another to my work presented in this thesis. First of all, my parents have always supported me during my studies and research and expressed their confidence in me. My supervisor, Prof. Dr. Hans Hagen, is the main reason that I was willing and able to conduct this work. He considered me for a position in his group long before I was even aware that I might and can pursue a PhD. Without his empowerment, I would probably never have thought I could be successful in research. He also provided an excellent an unmatched working environment in his group with the International Research Training Group (IRTG) 1131, which funded my research and enabled extensive collaborations with and travels to colleagues in Salt Lake City and Leipzig.

Long before I even finished my studies, Dr. Gerd Reis introduced me to visualization research with a focus on biomedical applications while supervising both my Bachelor's and Master's theses. He made it possible for me to work in exciting and novel research areas, publish the results, and learn many useful things from his expertise.

I have met many amazing and skilled medical researchers from the University Hospital of Leipzig, most notably Prof. Dr. Hermann Wrigge and especially PD Dr. Andreas Reske. Andreas guided my research with advice, suggestions, and excellent professional expertise. He is the most important link in this research collaboration since his experience both in medical and also computational engineering research enables him to fuse these two very different areas into a productive and promising collaboration. It was in fact Prof. Dr. Gerik Scheuermann from the University of Leipzig who initiated this work by introducing me to the medical researchers in Leipzig and thus providing me with an exciting and challenging research topic I could never even have dreamed of.

It cannot be stressed enough how important our group's secretary, Mady Gruys, is to the success of all the people working with Hans. She provides help and advice in all imaginable cases, cares about the many professional and personal worries and trouble, supports the ever so complicated and sometimes annoying struggle with university bureaucracy, and keeps everyone in our group sane and happy during difficult times.

I am deeply thankful to Kathrin Häb who has taken great effort to correct this text and suggest very helpful linguistic improvements, especially since I tend to produce very long sentences.

Finally, all my wonderful colleagues and friends supported me during the last couple of years, showed interest in my work, and gave a lot of encouraging and helpful advice.

My appreciation and thanks go to all these people who luckily played such an important role in my life and work.

Abstract

Mechanical ventilation of patients with severe lung injury is an important clinical treatment to ensure proper lung oxygenation and to mitigate the extent of collapsed lung regions. While current imaging technologies such as Computed Tomography (CT) and chest X-ray allow for a thorough inspection of the thorax, they are limited to static pictures and exhibit several disadvantages, including exposure to ionizing radiation and high cost. Electrical Impedance Tomography (EIT) is a novel method to determine functional processes inside the thorax such as lung ventilation and cardiac activity. EIT reconstructs the internal electrical conductivity distribution within the thorax from voltage measurements on the body surface. Conductivity changes correlate with important clinical parameters such as lung volume and perfusion. Current EIT systems and algorithms use simplified or generalized thorax models to solve the reconstruction problem, which reduce image quality and anatomical significance. In this thesis, the development of a clinically relevant workflow to compute sophisticated three-dimensional thorax models from patient-specific CT data is described. The method allows medical experts to generate a multi-material segmentation in an interactive and fast way, while a volumetric mesh is computed automatically from the segmentation. The significantly improved image quality and anatomical precision of EIT images reconstructed with these 3D models is reported, and the impact on clinical applicability is discussed. In addition, three projects concerning quantitative CT (qCT) measurements and multi-modal 3D visualization are presented, which demonstrate the importance and productivity of interdisciplinary research groups including computer scientists and medical experts. The results presented in this thesis contribute significantly to clinical research efforts to pave the way towards improved patient-specific treatments of lung injury using EIT and qCT.

Zusammenfassung

Die mechanische Beatmung von Patienten mit ernsten Lungenschäden ist eine wichtige klinische Behandlungsmethode, um eine ausreichende Oxygenierung der Lunge zu gewährleisten und um das Ausmaß von kollabierten Lungenregionen zu reduzieren. Während derzeitige Bildgebungstechnologien wie Computertomographie (CT) und Röntgenaufnahmen eine sorgfältige Untersuchung des Thorax ermöglichen, sind sie auf statische Bilder beschränkt und weisen einige Nachteile auf, darunter die Aussetzung von ionisierender Strahlung und hohe Kosten. Elektrische Impedanztomographie (EIT) ist eine neuartige Methode, um funktionale Prozesse innerhalb des Thorax, wie beispielsweise Lungenbelüftung und Herzaktivität, zu bestimmen. EIT rekonstruiert die Verteilung der elektrischen Leitfähigkeit innerhalb des Thorax aus Spannungsmessungen an der Körperoberfläche. Leitfähigkeitsänderungen korrelieren mit wichtigen klinischen Parametern wie Lungenvolumen und Durchblutung. Derzeitige EIT-Systeme und Algorithmen benutzen vereinfachte oder generalisierte Modelle des Thorax, um das Rekonstruktionsproblem zu lösen, was die Bildqualität und die anatomische Aussagekraft reduziert. In dieser Arbeit wird die Entwicklung eines klinisch relevanten Arbeitsablaufs zur Erzeugung von anspruchsvollen dreidimensionalen Thoraxmodellen aus patienten-spezifischen CT-Daten beschrieben. Die Methode erlaubt es medizinischen Experten, interaktiv und schnell eine multi-materielle Segmentierung zu erstellen, während ein volumetrisches Tetraeder-Netz automatisch aus der Segmentierung berechnet wird. Es wird über die signifikant verbesserte Bildqualität und anatomische Präzision der EIT-Bilder, die mit diesen 3D-Modellen rekonstruiert werden, berichtet, und die Bedeutung für die klinische Anwendbarkeit wird diskutiert. Zusätzlich werden drei Projekte präsentiert, welche quantitative CT-Messungen (qCT) und multi-modale 3D-Visualisierung betreffen, und die die Wichtigkeit und Produktivität von interdisziplinären Forschungsgruppen, bestehend aus Informatikern und Ärzten, demonstrieren. Die Ergebnisse dieser Arbeit tragen signifikant zu Bemühungen der klinischen Forschung bei, den Weg zu einer patienten-spezifischen Behandlung von Lungenschäden mit Hilfe von EIT und qCT zu ebnen.

Contents

1 Introduction   1
    1.1 Medical Research Motivation 1
    1.2 Electrical Impedance Tomography 2
    1.3 Collaboration 2
    1.4 Research Question and Goals 3
    1.5 Contributions and Significance 4
    1.6 Structure of the Dissertation 6

2 Medical Imaging of the Lung   7
    2.1 Computed Tomography (CT) 7
    2.2 Electrical Impedance Tomography 8
    2.3 State of the Clinical Application 14
    2.4 Challenges 14

3 Related and Prior Work   19
    3.1 Prior Work in Medicine (CT and EIT) 19
    3.2 EIT Models 24
    3.3 EIT Image Interpretation 28

4 CT Segmentation   31
    4.1 Research Question and Goal 32
    4.2 Differentiation from Related Work 34
    4.3 Proposed Segmentation Workflow 38
    4.4 Results 56
    4.5 Significance for Clinical Research 58
    4.6 Outlook 59

5	**Three-dimensional EIT Models**		**61**
	5.1	Generation of Finite Element Models from the Segmentation	62
	5.2	Final EIT Model using EIDORS	66
	5.3	Summary	70
	5.4	Outlook	72
6	**EIT Image Reconstruction and Interpretation**		**75**
	6.1	Reconstruction using EIDORS and GREIT	76
	6.2	Comparison to the State of Research	79
	6.3	Novel Insights due to the 3D Models	82
	6.4	Impact on EIT Analysis Methods	84
	6.5	Landmark Detection and Registration with CT	86
	6.6	Outlook	92
7	**Additional Collaborations with Medical Researchers**		**95**
	7.1	Ten Slice Extrapolation	96
	7.2	Study concerning CT subvolume regions of interest	104
	7.3	Development of a CT Segmentation Platform	120
8	**Visual and Quantitative Comparison of EIT Models**		**127**
	8.1	Research Question and Goal	127
	8.2	Utilized Data Sets	130
	8.3	Model Generation	131
	8.4	Image Reconstruction	135
	8.5	Quantitative Comparison	138
	8.6	Results	142
	8.7	Conclusion	145
9	**3D Visualization of CT, EIT, and Segmentation Data**		**149**
	9.1	Research Question and Goal	150
	9.2	Utilized Data Sets	151
	9.3	Visualization Techniques and Design Choices	153
	9.4	Implementation	157
	9.5	Results	158
	9.6	Future Work	160

10 Future Work and Conclusion 161
10.1 Future Work 161
10.2 Conclusion 165

Chapter 1

Introduction

This chapter gives an overview of the medical research questions that arise from Electrical Impedance Tomography imaging. Our extensive collaboration with medical experts is introduced, and the research goals and contributions of this thesis are described.

1.1 Medical Research Motivation

Mechanical ventilation is a routine procedure in clinical practice for patients in the intensive care unit (ICU), but also during surgery or other treatments. Trauma patients with severe lung injury often require a full replacement of breathing activity, while mild cases can be treated by assisting spontaneous breathing.

In addition to ensuring sufficient aeration and oxygenation of the lung, mechanical ventilation is also used to treat lung damage, such as the Acute Respiratory Distress Syndrome (ARDS), also known as shock lung. By performing delicate ventilation-related maneuvers, it is possible to open previously collapsed lung regions such that they contribute again to the lung function. Another challenge for clinicians is to monitor and control the regional ratio of ventilation and perfusion, since aerated lung regions without proper blood supply cannot contribute to oxygenation.

As endotracheal tubes cause a high risk of inflammation or injury of the bronchia, a main goal of mechanical ventilation is to minimize the time of their necessity. Also, parameter selection and tuning for ventilation such as volume or pressure of inhaled gas is very challenging. The values should be chosen in such a way to maximize the usefulness of the maneuver, while simultaneously minimizing the risk of exposing the patient to additional injuries.

The most common imaging tools for thorax trauma patients are Computed Tomography (CT) and chest X-ray. Especially CT data provides a large spatial resolution with high anatomical precision and a 3D representation of the thorax. Unfortunately, it exposes the patient to significant amounts of ionizing radiation, is costly, requires transportation of the patient, and only produces static images which do not cover functional processes.

Hence, there is a need for a cheap and time-dynamic imaging technique that does not emit harmful radiation, can be applied at bedside, and is thus suitable for severely injured patients in the ICU.

1.2 Electrical Impedance Tomography

Electrical Impedance Tomography (EIT) is a technology which has been studied in research for several decades, but only recently started to become of practical use for patient treatment. EIT is based on reconstructing internal conductivity distributions and changes from voltage measurements taken on the body surface. These conductivity changes correlate strongly with clinically relevant parameters such as lung volume and perfusion. EIT fulfills the requirements stated above, but for its clinical usefulness, detailed prior information concerning patient geometry and conductivity distribution is needed to reduce artifacts, distortions and errors.

1.3 Collaboration

The work presented in this thesis is based on a very productive and successful collaboration with the Clinic and Policlinic for Anesthesiology and Intensive Care Medicine at the University Hospital of Leipzig. Prof. Dr. Hermann Wrigge and PD Dr. Andreas Reske from this group have excellent experience in conducting animal experiments involving pigs and sheep to study the effect of certain injuries on the lung as well as mechanical ventilation and treatment. They are also extensively involved in patient treatment in the ICU.

Furthermore, Prof. Dr. Gerik Scheuermann from the University of Leipzig supports this research collaboration with his expertise in medical visualization and image processing.

We also worked with the group of Prof. Dr. Rob MacLeod as well as with Prof. Dr. Charles Hansen and Mark Kim from the Scientific Computing and Imaging (SCI) Institute at the University of Utah in Salt Lake City (USA) on volumetric mesh generation from multi-material segmentations.

Finally, I conceived, designed, and supervised a Bachelor's thesis by Christina Gillmann at the University of Kaiserslautern.

1.4 Research Question and Goals

The overall goal of this work is to improve the anatomical significance of EIT images of the thorax. Current realizations of EIT image reconstruction methods rely on simplified or generalized models of thorax geometry and a homogeneous internal conductivity distribution. This significantly reduces image quality and interpretability of EIT to an extent that clinically useful applications are very rare.

We identified the need for patient-specific, three-dimensional body models which include a precise representation of internal organs and their conductivity. Although their necessity for clinically relevant EIT imaging is commonly acknowledged in the literature [3, 72], 3D models from patient-specific CT data are considered difficult to generate and computationally expensive. Also, the generation of such models from clinical imagery in the presence of severe lung pathologies requires a well-defined workflow and interactive image processing and segmentation tools which are usable by medical experts.

This thesis aims at developing a workflow to interactively generate 3D thorax models with complex geometry from patient-specific CT data, adapt state-of-the-art EIT image reconstruction methods to these novel models, and study the improved anatomical correspondence of these functional images with organ shapes and locations.

In addition, the close collaboration with medical experts spawned several smaller projects which involve anatomical analysis of quantitative CT (qCT) measurements to improve diagnostics and treatment planning of lung injuries.

These efforts are closely linked to EIT imaging, since qCT methods can facilitate the verification and validation of findings from EIT. Furthermore, insights concerning representative subsets of CT thorax data for qCT analysis can readily be applied to EIT thorax models. Our research goals are summarized in Figure 1.1.

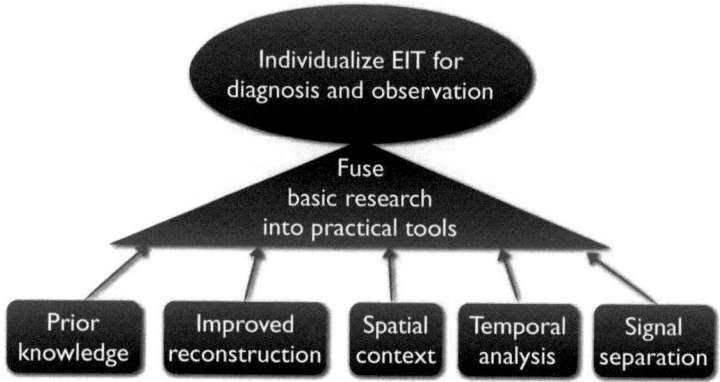

Figure 1.1: Our long term goals for individualized EIT imaging.

1.5 Contributions and Significance

Our proposed workflow consists of several central steps. The first is to generate a multi-material segmentation of a patient's CT scan in a fast, comprehensible and interactive way. We developed a semi-automatic segmentation procedure to enable medical researchers to determine the lung shape and other structures much faster and more easily than with the current manual approach. The method requires reduced interactive input by the user for difficult steps, such as discriminating pathological lung parts from surrounding tissue. The method's core is a known algorithm based on geodesic distances and statistical properties collected from user-drawn sparse sketches. Figure 1.2 depicts a 3D segmentation of a human thorax with several organs as generated by our workflow.

This volume mask is then converted to a tetrahedral Finite Element Mesh with multiple materials and mesh refinements near the EIT electrodes and

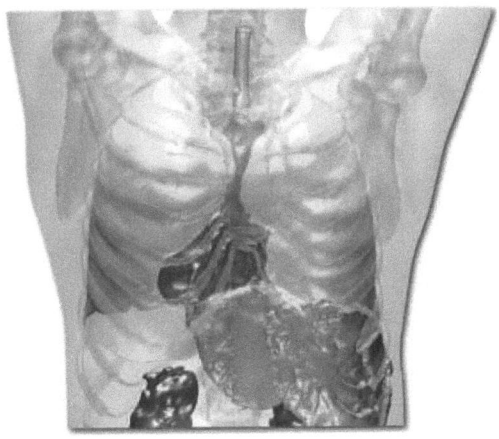

Figure 1.2: A segmented CT data set of a human thorax. The lungs (yellow), heart (red), liver (orange), kidneys (purple) and bones (white) are visualized as boundary surfaces.

material boundaries. Based on this mesh, a forward and inverse model is developed, taking into account prior information about the conductivity distribution, which can be used for EIT image reconstruction. The time-dynamic signals originating from breathing and cardiac activity can be separated and used to detect time-invariant landmarks such as the heart, the aorta and the main bronchia. We discuss a registration of these landmarks in both CT and EIT data to evaluate distortions in the images and to assess the anatomical correspondence of organ locations.

An evaluation study compares the anatomical precision of EIT images from our 3D models to state-of-the-art images in terms of overlap with a reference CT shape. While we can report a slightly superior lung and heart overlap precision of our patient-specific 3D models, we conclude that the current method to calculate this overlap is not suited for this kind of analysis and propose a different research direction for future work.

Two studies conducted by our medical collaborators concerning qCT measurements are supported in terms of computational processing and analysis. This allows for a significant reduction of processing time and more experimentation to determine representative subsets of the thorax for qCT measurements.

During our collaboration, the need for an improved visual communication between medical and visualization researchers arose, which is addressed by developing an interactive 3D visualization of the 3D data, the multi-material segmentation, and the 2D EIT images using boundary surfaces and volume rendering with an improved transfer function based on the segmentation.

1.6 Structure of the Dissertation

We give a short introduction to medical imaging related to the lung and motivate Electrical Impedance Tomography in Chapter 2. Related work concerning EIT and CT in both clinical and computational research is summarized in Chapter 3.

The next chapters present our proposed workflow to generate three-dimensional patient-specific thorax models for EIT image reconstruction. In Chapter 4, a segmentation workflow is proposed which explicitly includes medical expert knowledge gained from interactive steps. This workflow produces a multi-material segmentation of the thorax in a fast and convenient way. In Chapter 5 , we describe how this segmentation is converted to a volumetric tetrahedral mesh. In Chapter 6 we show how this 3D model can in turn be used for EIT image reconstruction, report several novel findings due to this improved reconstruction, and outline the impact of our work for clinical research.

Chapter 7 covers three projects in collaboration with our medical experts regarding quantitative CT analysis and CT segmentation. We report on our study concerning the visual and quantitative comparison of EIT images reconstructed with our proposed workflow to the state-of-the-art in terms of anatomical overlap with CT data in Chapter 8. Chapter 9 is dedicated to a Bachelor thesis project under my supervision which tackles the challenging task of developing a multi-modal 3D visualization of CT data, a multi-material segmentation, and time-dynamic 2D EIT images.

Finally, we summarize our contributions and outline future work in Chapter 10.

Chapter 2

Medical Imaging of the Lung

This chapter introduces common medical imaging techniques suitable for mechanical ventilation and treatment of lung injuries. We summarize Computed Tomography and Electrical Impedance Tomography, and give an overview of clinical applications and notable challenges.

2.1 Computed Tomography (CT)

Computed Tomography is routinely used in many clinical applications in addition to conventional X-ray imaging. A high-frequency beam of ionizing radiation traverses the body in a straight line, while the energy attenuation caused by objects along the path is measured by a detector. This combination of energy source and measurement detector is rotated around the body, thus generating detailed information about the internal matter. Using a back-projection algorithm, it is possible to reconstruct the internal density distribution with a large spatial resolution. The density is represented on the Hounsfield scale (HU), where water is assigned to the value 0 HU and air to -1000 HU.

The three-dimensional anatomical information is reconstructed onto transverse slices, which are exemplified in Figures 2.1 and 2.2. The first figure shows thorax slices from two human patients, one without (left) and one with a lung injury (right). Similarly, Figure 2.2 depicts CT data from a pig before (left) and after (right) an induced lung injury. The pig also wears an EIT measurement belt whose metal electrodes are shown as bright objects on the thorax boundary.

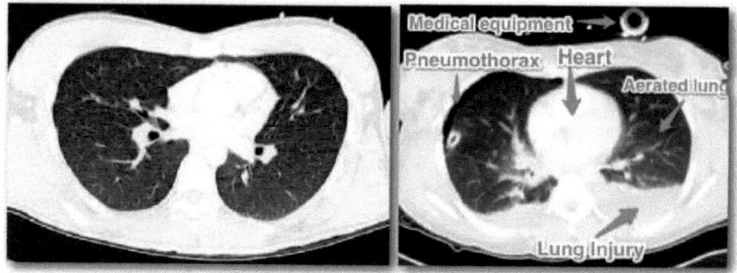

Figure 2.1: Representative CT slices from human patients with healthy (left) and diseased (right) lungs.

Several drawbacks and limitations of CT imaging are discussed in Chapter 2.4. Two of the most critical disadvantages are the patient's exposure to significant amounts of ionizing radiation and the necessity to transport the patient to the radiology department. This can be a risky or even life-threatening procedure for severely injured patients treated at the Intensive Care Unit (ICU).

In Figure 2.3, we give an overview of human (a) and pig (b) body geometry generated from the CT data.

2.2 Electrical Impedance Tomography

The EIT Problem

In contrast to Computed Tomography, EIT imaging attempts to approximate the internal conductivity distribution of a body from voltage measurements on the body's boundary. In most applications, a set of electrodes is attached to the body forming a transverse plane. Electric current patterns are applied to one (usually adjacent) pair of electrodes, and the resulting boundary voltages are measured at all other electrodes. This pattern is then rotated until measurements for all electrode pairs are taken, resulting in 208 measurements for 16 electrodes at a single time step. Interestingly, although almost always referred to as impedance tomography in the literature, EIT does not deliver tomographic images on a slice-by-slice basis such as CT. Different to the high-frequency radiation beam in CT, low frequency electric currents which are

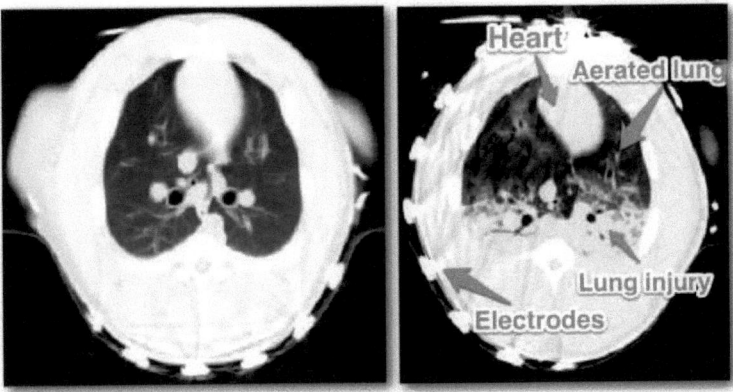

Figure 2.2: Representative CT slices from a pig before (left) and after (right) an induced lung injury.

injected into the body and measured on the surface in a single plane will traverse the body non-linearly and in all three dimensions.

The main motivation for EIT imaging of the thorax is the correlation of thoracic conductivity changes to physiological processes, such as change of lung volume and perfusion. From inspiration to expiration, a conductivity change of about 300% in the lungs has been found, and perfusion-related conductivity changes of about 3% during the cardiac cycle are determined. More details on electrical properties of body tissue are given by Hyttinen et al. [87] and Faes et al. [53]. Brown [25] presents a detailed review about EIT-related research. Figure 2.4(a) shows the conductivity change during mechanical ventilation, averaged over all image pixels. The high-frequency variations are attributed to perfusion.

Mathematically, Electrical Impedance Tomography is very difficult to handle, which is the reason for the rather slow advancement towards practical applications. The mathematical properties of EIT are exhaustively covered by Hanke-Burgeois [81]. Since these are not the main focus of this thesis, only a very short introduction is given, following the excellent descriptions by Holder [84]. The governing equations are Ohm's law for the current density $\mathbf{J}$ and the electric field $\mathbf{E}$, where ϕ is the electric scalar potential and σ the conductivity

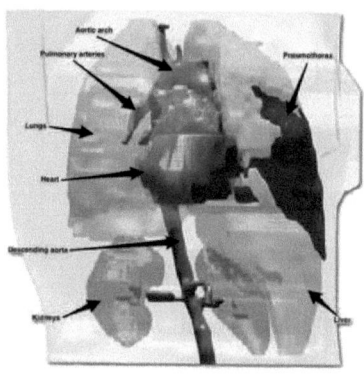 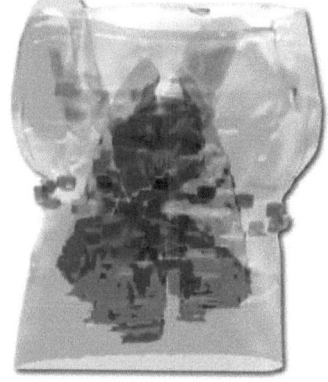

(a) Detailed segmentation of a human thorax.

(b) Segmentation of a pig's thorax including lung pathology (purple).

Figure 2.3: Exemplary 3D visualization of segmentations from human and pig thorax CT data.

in a body Ω:

$$\mathbf{E} = -\nabla \phi \qquad (2.1)$$
$$\mathbf{J} = -\sigma \nabla \phi \qquad (2.2)$$

and Kirchhoff's law:

$$\nabla \cdot \sigma \nabla \phi = 0. \qquad (2.3)$$

The current density j on the boundary surface $\partial \Omega$ with unit normal $\mathbf{n}$ can then be determined as:

$$j = \sigma \nabla \phi \cdot \mathbf{n} \qquad (2.4)$$

Together with the conditions $\int_{\partial \Omega} j = 0$ and $\int_{\partial \Omega} \phi = 0$, this equation forms the so-called continuum model. Since only a finite set of measurements is taken at discrete electrode locations on the boundary surface, j is not completely known in practice. Hence, this model is commonly replaced by the

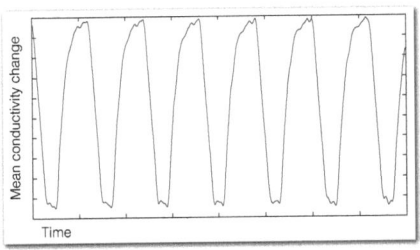 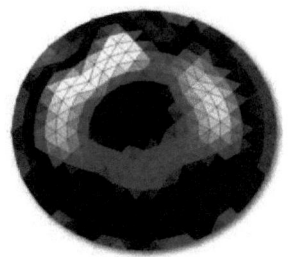

(a) Mean conductivity change in the thorax during mechanical ventilation. The high-frequency components are related to cardiac activity.

(b) An EIT image reconstructed onto a circular grid.

Figure 2.4: Examples of typical EIT data and early image reconstructions.

Complete Electrode Model. Here, the electrode shape is precisely modeled, and the surface impedance z_l for electrode l ($l = 1, ..., L$), representing the highly resistive layer between the electrode and the surface, is also considered (assuming a voltage measurement V_l):

$$\phi + z_l \sigma \frac{\partial \phi}{\partial \mathbf{n}} = V_l. \tag{2.5}$$

It has been proven by Somersalo et al. [149] that the Complete Electrode Model has an existent and unique solution.

The inverse EIT reconstruction problem consists of estimating the internal conductivity distribution σ (or the complex admittivity $\gamma = \sigma + i\omega\epsilon$, with ω being the angular frequency of the applied current pattern, and ϵ the permittivity) from boundary voltage measurements V_l. The forward problem, specified by a non-linear forward operator F, is $\mathbf{V} = F(\sigma)$, which involves solving the Laplace equation 2.3.

As summarized by Holder [84], this is considered a severely ill-posed inverse problem, according to Hadamard's conditions for a well-posed problem, which require the existence and uniqueness of a solution that depends continuously on the data. Especially the third condition poses severe practical problems, since almost arbitrarily large conductivity changes cannot be reconstructed from the boundary measurements. However, as described below, prior information about the conductivity distribution can render the problem feasible again.

Image Reconstruction

Several early attempts have been made to measure impedance in the thorax, such as by Henderson and Webster [83] and by Kim et al. [93]. In the latter publication, a numerical solution to Laplace's equation is proposed, and a back-projection algorithm is used to reconstruct images. Barber and Brown [13] were the first to publish impedance images of the human forearm. They perform a back-projection along equi-potential lines in the measurement plane for image reconstruction. A visual example of this approach is given by Teschner and Imhoff [152].

An overview of early EIT image reconstruction approaches is presented by Barber [12] and Breckon [24].

In the following, we loosely use the notation by Adler et al. [3] and Holder [84]. Difference (or dynamic) EIT imaging involves normalized difference data $\mathbf{y}$ calculated from voltage measurements V and a reference voltage V_r:

$$\mathbf{y} = \frac{V - V_r}{V_r} \qquad (2.6)$$

The forward operator which maps internal conductivity to boundary voltages can be linearized such that

$$F(\sigma) \approx F(\sigma_0) + \mathbf{J}\left(\sigma - \sigma_0\right). \qquad (2.7)$$

Here, σ_0 is an initial estimate of the conductivity, and $\mathbf{J}$ is the Jacobian, also called sensitivity matrix which contains the derivatives of voltage measurements with respect to the conductivity. Generally, this kind of equation can be approximately solved by a replacement of the least squares approach, the so-called Tikhonov regularization. Assuming a system of equations $\mathbf{A}\mathbf{x} = \mathbf{b}$, the Tikhonov regularization solution is

$$\mathbf{x}_\alpha = \arg\min_x \|\mathbf{A}\mathbf{x} - \mathbf{b}\|^2 + \alpha^2 \|\mathbf{x}\| \qquad (2.8)$$

with a regularization parameter α. Following the slightly different notation by Adler et al. [3], where impedance changes are calculated as

$$\hat{\mathbf{x}} = \mathbf{R}\mathbf{y} \qquad (2.9)$$

from the linearization $\mathbf{y} = \mathbf{Jx} + \mathbf{n}$, where $\mathbf{n}$ is the measurement noise, modeled as uncorrelated white Gaussian noise, the reconstruction matrix $\mathbf{R}$ can be determined by minimizing the generalized Tikhonov regularization

$$\|\mathbf{y} - \mathbf{J}\hat{\mathbf{x}}\|^2_{\Sigma_\mathbf{n}^{-1}} + \|\mathbf{x} - \mathbf{x}^0\|^2_{\Sigma_\mathbf{x}^{-1}}. \tag{2.10}$$

The expected value $\mathbf{x}^0$ is zero for difference imaging. Furthermore, $\Sigma_\mathbf{n}^{-1}$ is the covariance of the noise and $\Sigma_\mathbf{x}^{-1}$ is the covariance of the expected image. Defining a priori information $\mathbf{V} = \sigma_n^2 \Sigma_n$ (σ_n^2 is the averaged measurement noise amplitude) and $\mathbf{P} = \sigma_x^2 \Sigma_x$ (σ_x^2 is the prior amplitude of conductivity change), the one-step inverse solution is then

$$\hat{\mathbf{x}} = \left(\mathbf{J}^T \mathbf{V}^{-1} \mathbf{J} + \alpha^2 \mathbf{P}^{-1}\right)^{-1} \mathbf{J}^T \mathbf{V}^{-1} \mathbf{y}. \tag{2.11}$$

Finally, the reconstruction matrix can be written in the Wiener filter form

$$\mathbf{R} = \mathbf{P}\mathbf{J}^T \left(\mathbf{J}\mathbf{P}\mathbf{J}^T + \alpha^2 \mathbf{V}\right)^{-1}. \tag{2.12}$$

A similar solution, where the diagonal of the prior matrix is scaled with the sensitivity, i.e. $[\mathbf{P}^{-1}]_{i,i} = [\mathbf{J}^T \mathbf{J}]_{i,i}$, is presented by Cheney et al. [33] as the Newton's One-Step Error Reconstructor (NOSER).

Note that an analytical solution of this problem is only possible for a very simple geometry, such as a circle, and for an (almost) homogeneous conductivity distribution. The solution above also is only useful for very small deviations from the reference or background conductivity. Since in practice we experience significant changes in the thorax during breathing and other processes, this solution causes severe errors and poor image quality. Commonly, the solution is numerically calculated on a finite element grid [168]. Confer Figure 2.4(b) for an EIT image reconstructed on a circular mesh with homogeneous background conductivity.

The state-of-the-art linear reconstruction algorithm *GREIT* [3] is described in Chapter 3.

Several attempts have been made to measure absolute electrical impedance in the thorax [45, 79]. This proves to be much more difficult than difference imaging, since the uncertainties from inaccurate shape modeling, electrode impedance, and prior information about the conductivity distribution introduce very critical artifacts and decrease image quality significantly.

2.3 State of the Clinical Application

Computed Tomography and X-ray imagery are routinely used in clinical practice, especially for thorax trauma patients. They are usually visually inspected by the radiologist or another medical expert to assess pathologies and to derive treatment strategies. Particularly with regard to 3D, hardly any further image processing or visualization of the data is performed. Also, quantitative CT calculations are currently investigated in clinical research, but they are not yet routinely used in practice.

Notable commercial products involving Electrical Impedance Tomography are the PulmoVista 500 by Dräger [152] and the very recent BB^2 by Swisstom [17]. The Dräger device is used for bedside monitoring of mechanical ventilation with a visual representation of the conductivity changes and a region of interest based plot of the temporal curves. No further image processing or interpretation is performed at bedside. Also, the baseline for image reconstruction is updated automatically over time. This prevents a meaningful interpretation of two ventilation states, such as before and after a certain treatment for the improvement of regional lung ventilation.

Other potential clinical applications are reviewed by Frerichs [58], Putensen et al. [123], Bodenstein et al. [16], Moerer et al. [109], Adler et al. [2], Wrigge and Reske [169], Frerichs [59], and Leonhardt [97].

2.4 Challenges

Computed Tomography

Although Computed Tomography features a very good spatial resolution and has been proven to correlate well with clinically relevant measurements (confer for example Reske et al. [130, 131, 129]), it has some relevant drawbacks. First of all, image quality can be severely decreased by high-density objects such as bones and metal. As depicted in Figure 2.2 (right), the metal electrodes on the thorax surface cause streaking and dark band artifacts as well as partial volume effects. Other limitations concerning image normalization are summarized by Horwood et al. [85].

While CT data is routinely used for the treatment of lung damage, the image slices are usually visually inspected without any computational processing. Clinicians are trained to derive diagnoses and patient treatment strategies from the images, and to recognize and work around image errors and artifacts. However, three-dimensional relations between volume regions or objects cannot be optimally grasped by two-dimensional visualizations. Many 3D visualizations applying volume rendering and boundary surfaces have been proposed over the last decades, but they are commonly rejected by medical experts due to the large degree of abstraction and the disregard of the original image data (confer for example Karimov et al. [88]).

A major challenge of CT imaging is the segmentation of certain structures or objects of interest. While some structures, such as bones or the aerated lung, can easily be distinguished from surrounding material by thresholding the Hounsfield scale, many soft tissues have very similar density values. In terms of lung imaging, poorly or non-aerated lung tissue is very difficult to discriminate from other soft tissue. Significant medical experience is required to notice these delicate boundaries (confer Figure 2.1 (right)). Therefore, the state-of-the-art process in clinical practice is to manually delineate the lung boundary, especially in the dorsal region, which is very time-consuming. Also, inspection is necessary to account for possible errors during the process. Many automated algorithms have been proposed to speed up the segmentation, but they commonly fail in the presence of severe pathologies or artifacts and are thus neglected in clinical practice.

Using the vendor's proprietary processes, CT image slices are usually generated from raw data, which is discarded afterwards. These processes include interpolation and smoothing, while the necessary parameters are not available for post-processing. Several methods for artifact reduction work on the raw data. Since this data is not available, the image reconstruction can still be inverted, but due to the unknown parameters from the original process, this results in loss of image quality. Reske et al. [128] show that quantitative CT measurements are only comparable if identical reconstruction parameters were used.

Finally, 3D calculations as well as image interpretation are challenging due to the anisotropic spatial resolution of CT image data. The slice thickness, i.e. the distance between individual image slices, can typically be ten times as

Figure 2.5: Visualization of a segmented pig's thorax highlighting the large vertical voxel anisotropy. Ribs (brown), heart (red), aorta (green), pulmonary arteries (pink), atelectatic lung tissue (yellow) are shown.

large as the pixel size. Common settings in clinical practice are a pixel area of 0.6×0.6 mm^2 and a slice thickness of $3 - 10$ mm. Figure 2.5 depicts a visualization of a thorax segmentation from a pig, indicating the blocky and anisotropic voxel size. In medical visualization and image processing, these artifacts are commonly smoothed, but this also results in loss and distortion of original image information.

Electrical Impedance Tomography

As described before, EIT is a severely ill-posed inverse problem from a mathematical point of view. Even without real-world obstacles in practice, this problem is difficult to solve. Most critically, prior information about the geometry of the body (boundary shape, lung shape, electrode positions and contact impedance) and the internal conductivity distribution are necessary to mitigate the most severe artifacts and image errors [21, 74, 70]. Additionally, it can be concluded that the commonly applied adjacent current patterns significantly decrease image quality [4]. Since the currents traverse the body in 3D, the resulting EIT images reflect a projection of the three-dimensional conductivity distribution into the measurement plane. While this hampers the anatomical interpretability by itself, Zhao et al. [178] showed that the lung regions contributing to the EIT image depend on the position of the measurement plane.

The dorsal lung boundary is one of the most important regions for clinical researchers to determine the effect of certain treatments to mitigate lung collapse (atelectasis). Without additional anatomical context, it is almost impossible to distinguish those lung pixels from surrounding pixels, since both exhibit almost no conductivity change during ventilation. Hence, most EIT image interpretation methods only estimate the lung boundary, which reduces the medical significance.

Many sources contribute to the conductivity changes inside the thorax in addition to the lungs and the heart. Since they are usually not modeled, uncertainty is always involved when interpreting EIT images. As reported by Proença et al. [119], the heart motion contributes strongly to the EIT image, especially when monitoring perfusion.

The low image resolution of EIT causes several artifacts such as partial volume effects, and detecting or locating small conductivity changes is very difficult.

To improve the anatomical significance of EIT, the general consensus is to use patient-specific three-dimensional thorax models [3, 72], but it is complicated and time-consuming to generate these.

Chapter 3

Related and Prior Work

Since this work tackles several research areas and clinical applications, we first give an overview of prior efforts concerning the practical applicability of Electrical Impedance Tomography for mechanical ventilation (Chapter 3.1). First approaches for EIT-based perfusion analysis are also covered, as well as early attempts to develop quantitative CT measures.

Approaches for CT segmentation which influence our own work will be detailed in Chapter 4.

The state-of-the-art in EIT modeling and image reconstruction is summarized in Chapter 3.2, while publications on EIT image interpretation and analysis are presented in Chapter 3.3.

3.1 Prior Work in Medicine (CT and EIT)

Introduction to Mechanical Ventilation and Lung Treatment

Mechanical ventilation, i.e. the assistance of spontaneous breathing or the complete replacement of breathing activity, is applied to many patients in clinical practice. Our research collaboration is mostly focused on the treatment of patients suffering from acute lung injury (ALI), also called acute respiratory distress syndrome (ARDS). Without considering many medical details, in summary ARDS patients suffer from progressive lung failure, which is a potentially life-threatening condition. Common causes are pneumonia (inflammation of the airway or lung tissue), blunt thorax trauma from accidents, and traumatic brain injury. Mechanical ventilation is usually performed by placing an endotracheal tube inside the upper airways (main bronchus), letting oxygenated air flow into the lungs and transporting used gas out of the body. During this process, either the volume or the pressure is controlled. For volume controlled ventilation, the inhaled air volume is fixed, while pressure controlled ventilation specifies a constant pressure inside the lungs. Confer for example [169] for more details and references.

The most important challenge for medical experts is to minimize the duration of mechanical ventilation. This is due to several reasons, such as the progressive weakening of breathing-related muscles and the increased risk of ventilator-induced lung injury (VALI). VALI can be caused by either the endotracheal tube (inflammation or physical injury of the airways), or by the process of mechanical ventilation itself, resulting for example in overdistension of lung tissue or progressive collapse of (mostly dorsal) lung regions. Also, continuous medication is usually necessary to enable the patient to accept the invasive presence of the tube. Delicate optimization of ventilation parameters such as tidal volume, positive end-expiratory pressure (PEEP) or inspiration flow is required to aerate the patient sufficiently and to minimize the risk of VALI.

In addition to the aeration of the lung, another purpose of mechanical ventilation is the treatment of lung injury. There are several ventilation-related lung pathologies which require different treatment strategies. Collapsed lung regions, also called atelectasis, do not contribute to the gas exchange. Due to the supine position of most patients, these occur mostly in the dorsal lung region. Emphysema are irreversible overdistensions of the lung alveoli, causing a loss of elasticity of the lung. Pleural effusion of fluids into the pleural space between the ribs and the lung causes dyspnea. A special case of pleural effusion is the hematothorax where blood fills the pleural space due to a blunt thorax trauma or other injuries. Finally, a pneumothorax, i.e. the leaking of gas into the pleural space, is a life-threatening condition if a rupture of the lung allows leaking of air during each breath without reflux. This can result in a rapid compression and collapse of the lung. Typically, a pneumothorax is caused by the penetration of the lung by broken ribs or sharp objects such as knives and bullets, or by a hyper-ventilation with dangerously increased volume or pressure of inhaled air.

Clinicians have several options to treat these severe thorax injuries with mechanical ventilation. To avoid overdistension caused by too much pressure, or atelectasis due to low, but lung-protective pressure, a common strategy is the PEEP titration. Step by step, the PEEP level is increased over a certain period of time until the lung is completely opened during inspiration. Then, the PEEP is decreased again until an optimal ventilation setting is found which avoids regional lung collapse after each expiration. Another option for lung recruitment is the lowflow maneuver, where a large amount of air slowly fills the lung with constant flow. Pleural effusions can be drained by surgically placing drainage tubes inside the pleural cavity. Similarly, the leaked air causing a pneumothorax is drained, requiring a precise localization and X-ray guided insertion of the drainage tubes through the space between the ribs.

Providing the lung with oxygenated air is not sufficient for a proper lung function. In order for the gas exchange to succeed at the alveoli, perfusion of the respective organs is critically important. The regional ratio between ventilation and perfusion, the so-called V/Q matching, needs to be intensively monitored, especially in atelectatic regions. Omitting medical details, lung regions which hardly or not at all contribute to the gas exchange, experience a decreased perfusion due to rerouting of the blood flow or vessel damage. Thus, even if these regions are opened during a recruitment maneuver with sufficiently large PEEP, the non-optimal V/Q matching can cause an insufficient oxygenation.

These regional lung characteristics cannot be easily monitored or quantified by common imaging techniques such as CT or X-ray. Also, these methods expose the patient to significant amounts of ionizing radiation and they are costly. Often, the patient has to be transported to the radiology department, which is risky and inconvenient for patients in the intensive care unit (ICU).

In the following, we summarize attempts to use Electrical Impedance Tomography as an imaging technique and monitoring device for the treatment of mechanically ventilated patients.

Clinical Applications of EIT

Frerichs [58] provides an excellent review of early clinical applications of EIT from the beginning of EIT research in the mid-1980s to the late 1990s. Putensen et al. [123] report improved regional ventilation and reduced alveolar collapse in patients with respiratory dysfunction after EIT-guided ventilator parameter adjustment. Wrigge et al. [170] compare functional EIT measurements to morphological CT data during a lowflow maneuver in pigs and determine that the regional ventilation delay correlates with recruitable lung volume. This delay of regional impedance change to reach a specified threshold, such as 40% of the maximal impedance change, is later studied by Muders et al. [111] as the regional ventilation delay (RVD) index.

Pulletz et al. [122] study the selection of regions of interest (ROI) to quantify regional lung ventilation, since pixel-by-pixel calculations are error-prone and unstable due to the low image resolution and strong noise signals. They conclude that a ROI boundary at 20-35% of the maximal standard deviation of impedance change is better suited than arbitrary shapes such as four evenly spaced quadrants.

The global airway pressure values which cause lung tissue to either open or close are estimated by Pulletz et al. [121] in a clinical study. They found significantly higher opening pressures for injured patients compared to healthy subjects and conclude that this index is potentially useful for determining optimal PEEP settings.

Pressure-volume curves in different lung regions during inflation and deflation are determined using EIT by Frerichs et al. [60]. They determine characteristic landmarks on these curves to be useful for mechanical ventilation guidance.

Wolf et al. [167] use EIT to measure regional lung volume during the treatment of lung collapse in children suffering from ALI. This is a very promising application area for EIT, since exposure of children to ionizing radiation caused by CT or X-ray imaging should be minimized.

These publications hint at the potential usefulness of EIT imaging for monitoring and guidance during lung treatment using quantitative information.

First commercial devices by Dräger [152] and Swisstom [17] are described below.

Quantitative CT Analysis

Computed Tomography scans are routinely used for ALI patients. Often, multiple scans over a period of several days or weeks are available. However, in clinical practice, these data sets are commonly only visually inspected in a slice-by-slice manner. The valuable numerical and morphological information contained in CT data is almost completely neglected due to the rather large computational efforts and the lack of clinical protocols. Only few clinical research publications tackle this area and are summarized here.

Malbouisson et al. [104] perform a successful validation study for the volume of water inside the lungs measured with CT data. While usually not available in clinical practice due to radiation exposure, cost, time, and data storage issues, Zaporozhan et al. [175] use thin-slice CT scans (1 mm inter-slice distance) from expiration and inspiration to determine lung volume, emphysema volume, and other indices related to emphysema. Similarly, Fuld et al. [62] measure specific lung volume change from sheep CT data.

Reske et al. [128] show that qCT measurements, here the volume of hyperinflated lung tissue, depends significantly on the parameters for CT image reconstruction. These parameters, such as the filter kernel used for smoothing, are mostly defined by the device manufacturer and their implementation details are often proprietary. Thus, qCT analyses are only comparable if the CT reconstruction settings are identical, which is difficult to achieve.

Häme et al. [80] propose a novel computational method based on Hidden Markov Measure Fields to determine an accurate segmentation of lung emphysema in CT scans. Raghunath et al. [124] study different CT reconstruction parameters to quantify pulmonary fibrosis and propose an approach to select the optimal settings.

Reske et al. [130, 131, 129] demonstrate that only ten evenly-spaced slices of the lung are sufficient to calculate representative qCT measurements such as volume and mass of normally, poorly or non-aerated lung tissue. This method is detailed in Chapter 7.1.

Finally, Camargo et al. [29] attempt to calculate the impeditivity of different tissues from CT scans to generate an anatomical atlas which can be used to improve Electrical Impedance Tomography.

3.2 EIT Models

Boundary Shape and Electrode Modeling

This section provides an overview of different thorax models for EIT image reconstruction. Early works until at least the mid-1990s used a circular model with homogeneous background conductivity due to computational constraints and easier mathematical handling. Borsic et al. [20] generate two-dimensional thorax meshes from a cryostatic image slice of the Visible Human Project. They consider the thorax, lung, and heart shape, but do not account for different organ conductivity priors. Due to discontinuities of the electric field at the boundary, a finer mesh density is required. Also, the mesh resolution is increased at the locations of the 32 electrodes, which are modeled using the Complete Electrode Model. The mesh center is much coarser since the electric field is weaker. Similar models are still widely used.

In a different approach, Nissinen et al. [114] acknowledge the missing patient-specific thorax information in clinical practice and attempt to compensate for the introduced modeling error. They use the approximation error approach which estimates the statistical characteristics of the error caused by incorrect boundary shape.

Grychtol et al. [74] extend the *GREIT* reconstruction algorithm proposed by Adler et al. [3] (see below) for arbitrary shapes. They develop a detailed forward model from a single CT slice incorporating thorax and lung shape as well as different conductivity settings for the lung compared to the background. Significantly improved results with reduced noise and artifacts, and better anatomical accuracy are reported.

It is a general consensus that fine meshes with complex shapes are necessary for improved EIT image quality and expressiveness. Also, 3D shapes are recommended over simple 2D meshes, as reported below. However, Adler and Lionheart [6] demonstrate the introduction of severe artifacts during image reconstruction when internal mesh elements are modified, for example to conform to a conductivity target. They hypothesize that this unexpected effect is due to anisotropic characteristics of the conductivity distribution which cannot be handled by the isotropic model. It is shown that large artifacts throughout the image occur, especially for three-dimensional fine meshes. A solution is proposed that includes a dedicated node movement term of the finite element model for the inverse formulation.

Boyle and Adler [21] conduct a simulation study to determine the effect of electrode modeling and boundary shape changes on EIT image quality. They investigate electrode area and contact impedance on the surface using the Complete Electrode Model. It is determined that an increased contact impedance removes many artifacts, while a low contact impedance is usually desired for optimal measurement sensitivity. Also, they conclude that area and contact impedance of electrodes as well as the boundary shape significantly influence EIT image artifacts.

In another study concerning model shape mismatch, Grychtol et al. [73] determine the error introduced by unrealistic thorax shapes. They conclude that small deviations from the true shape can be tolerated and that approximated models can reasonably substitute the real boundary shape. In a similar effort, Boyle et al. [22] study the effect of shape deformation and come to the same conclusion.

Three-dimensional Thorax Models

One of the first attempts to perform three-dimensional EIT imaging is reported by Metherall et al. [108]. They not only use a 3D mesh of a cylindrical measurement tank, but also record data from four planes containing 16 electrodes each. While this is a very promising approach for lung imaging, it is not practical for ICU use on severely injured patients.

Shortly before we started our work on patient-specific 3D thorax models, Fan and Wang [55] demonstrated the development of a sophisticated 3D thorax model involving thorax, lung and heart shape. They also include a specific material for collapsed dorsal lung regions. However, they do not provide a fast, generalizable and convenient way to construct these models. Furthermore, the heart shape is only approximated by an ellipsoid, and only simulated EIT measurements are provided to show the model's capabilities.

While EIT of the lungs is usually performed by difference imaging rather than by absolute conductivity measurements, other application areas require a very precise and anatomically accurate body model involving electrode shape, position and contact impedance as well as boundary shape. Tizzard et al.

[153] develop patient-specific 3D models to detect, locate and quantify breast cancer. This is achieved by adapting a template mesh to the actual breast shape.

A computationally inexpensive modeling approach is proposed by Bahrani and Adler [10]. They use so-called 2.5D models which are vertically invariant in terms of shape and conductivity distribution. Thus, modeling is only necessary in 2D, while a 3D mesh can easily be calculated. While not very accurate, the assumption of vertical homogeneity is a reasonable approximation in many applications. Even for a thorax model around the electrode belt, the thorax and lung shape are sufficiently invariant such that the 2.5D model is a good compromise between model accuracy and computational cost.

Shortly before we published our first results from patient-specific 3D models [138], Yang et al. [172] presented a very sophisticated thorax model calculated from an MR scan of a human subject. The data set is manually segmented into 36 different tissue types. Afterwards, they generate a volumetric mesh with almost four million elements and realistically model the different organ conductivities. This work demonstrates the superior EIT image quality using a very detailed model, but neither the number of different tissues, nor the manual segmentation are suited for clinical use.

Finally, Grychtol and Adler [71] present a way to automatically refine the mesh at the electrodes without distorting the boundary shape.

EIT Image Reconstruction

Soleimani et al. [147] demonstrate that it is possible to reconstruct electrode movement as well as conductivity change with EIT, thus reducing artifacts significantly.

The most commonly used stimulation and measurement pattern is adjacent injection and measurement. Adler et al. [4] show that this approach has very poor performance in terms of distinguishing conductivtiy distribution changes. They strongly recommend to use patterns which are separated between 90° and 180°.

Early attempts of EIT image reconstruction are summarized in a review by Barber [12]. Breckon [24] gives a thorough analysis of the mathematical properties of EIT reconstruction.

A reconstruction algorithm for 2D circular shapes which has been used for a long time is given by Cheney et al. [33]. The algorithm, called NOSER for Newton's One-Step Error Reconstructor, performs analytical computations based on Newton's method. The authors admit that only minimal deviations from a constant conductivity prior can be accurately reconstructed by this linearized algorithm. However, they argue that the resulting images appear useful, which has been a common argument during most of the 1990s.

An overview of reconstruction algorithms until the early 2000s is given by Lionheart [100]. Many approaches for forward solvers and reconstruction meshes are presented as well as algorithms based on regularization, linearization, backprojection, iteration, and also direct non-linear methods. Noise handling and how to avoid so-called "inverse crimes" is also mentioned.

Adler and Lionheart [5] present the *EIDORS* software framework which includes many reconstruction and analysis algorithms as well as mesh generation and shared data from clinical and animal studies.

One of the most influential developments in recent years is the Graz consensus reconstruction algorithm for EIT (*GREIT*) by Adler et al. [3]. As most experts related to the EIT technology contributed to this publication, the *GREIT* algorithm can be considered as de-facto standard for linearized reconstruction of difference imagery from EIT. One of the main contributions is the explicit use of 3D meshes for forward model calculations. Several meshes, such as an adult thorax model generated from the Visible Human Project and a neonate model, are included in the implementation which is integrated into *EIDORS*. To determine an optimal reconstruction matrix to map voltage measurements at the surface to internal conductivity changes, an equivalent approach to a generalized Tikhonov regularization is developed. The priors are influenced by noise models for electronic measurement noise and electrode movement, and by a training procedure to optimize certain figures of merit. Small conductivity targets are simulated inside the forward model by mesh deformation, and the reconstructed image is evaluated in terms of the figures of merit. These figures include amplitude response, position error, resolution, shape deformation, and ringing, which are visually illustrated in Figure 1 of [3]. This algorithm achieves significantly better results than the formerly used one-step Gauss-Newton or backprojection algorithms. Using the same notation as in Chapter 2.2, the *GREIT* reconstruction matrix can be expressed as

$$\mathbf{R}_{GR} = \tilde{\mathbf{X}}_t \mathbf{Y}_t^T \left(J\Sigma_x J^T + \Sigma_n \right)^{-1}. \tag{3.1}$$

The training data is represented by $\tilde{\mathbf{X}}_t$ and the measurement noise samples by $\mathbf{Y}_t$.

Zhao et al. [177] compare backprojection, *GREIT* using a circular model and *GREIT* using a patient-specific thorax shape in terms of image analysis. They conclude that while *GREIT* and anatomically realistic forward models improve EIT image quality and clinical acceptance, there is no significant difference concerning image analysis of linearity, global and regional ventilation distribution.

As mentioned in Chapter 2.3, one of the first commercial EIT devices, the PulmoVista 500 by Dräger [152], uses the linearized Newton-Raphson algorithm for image reconstruction. The forward model to determine the reconstruction matrix is averaged over many thorax CT scans from multiple patients. However, the inverse model is a severely simplified ellipsoid mesh with only 340 finite elements. The resulting 32×32 images are cleaned of boundary artifacts, smoothed by Gaussian filtering, and upscaled by bilinear filtering to be suited for visualization.

A recent competition product, BB^2 by Swisstom [17], uses 32 electrodes compared to the common 16 which are available in the Dräger device. Several 3D thorax models including lung and heart shape are directly stored on the device, and the most appropriate one is determined by several patient-specific parameters. The *GREIT* algorithm is used for reconstruction, and an accelerometer accounts for position changes of the patient.

3.3 EIT Image Interpretation

Adler et al. [2] summarize potential clinical use cases and report state-of-the-art EIT image analysis. Furthermore, they formulate several hypotheses regarding clinical applications, which are yet to be verified, although many recent works somewhat support these hypotheses. Leonhardt and Lachmann [98] provide a similar review.

An important finding concerning asymmetric images of symmetrically ventilated lungs is reported by Grychtol and Adler [70]. They determine the conductive heart, which is usually located on the left side of the thorax, to be the source of this asymmetry of the left lung, which can result in erroneous size increase of up to 60%. In a follow-up paper, Grychtol and Adler [72] show that the assumption of uniform background conductivity generally introduces large image errors. They come to the conclusion that patient-specific 3D forward models with large anatomical accuracy are necessary for EIT imaging to be useful and expressive.

A potentially useful ventilation strategy guide is proposed by Grychtol et al. [76]. They argue that, while values for inspiration and expiration pressure during mechanical ventilation can be deduced from the inflection points of the global pressure-volume curve, this does not properly reflect regional ventilation. Thus, they apply curve-fitting to local pressure-volume curves from EIT measurements.

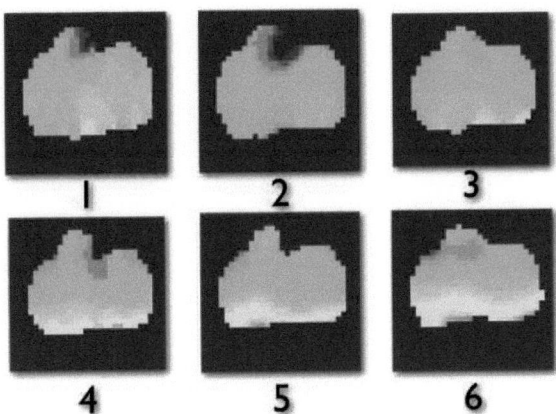

Figure 3.1: Standard deviation of the RVD index over time. Each picture represents a lowflow maneuver performed at different times. Red and orange colors indicate regions of increased inhomogeneity of the ventilation delay correlating with collapsed lung tissue.

Muders et al. [111] calculate recruitable lung regions during a lowflow maneuver, which is supposed to open almost all collapsed lung areas. A regional ventilation delay (RVD) index is computed which specifies the time delay for regional impedance changes to reach a level of 40% of the maximal value compared to the global change. They conclude that the standard deviation of this RVD is useful for identifying recruitable lung regions if a sufficient estimation of the dorsal lung boundary in the EIT data is available. Otherwise, severely collapsed lung pixel which do not exhibit a measurable RVD cannot be distinguished from non-lung pixels with the same behavior. We performed a similar calculation as presented in Figure 3.1. Over time, it is clearly visible how the induced lung damage in the pig causes increased amounts of atelectatic lung tissue for which tidal recruitment is more difficult.

Several more promising studies are summarized in Chapter 6.4, together with attempts to assess and quantify lung perfusion and cardiac activity by EIT imaging.

Chapter 4

CT Segmentation

Currently, most CT scans in clinical practice are only visually inspected by the radiologist or another physician. This is done by scrolling through the grayscale images slice by slice, while only the window of the grayscale range can be interactively modified to highlight different densities and to change brightness and contrast. In clinical research, however, segmentation of the lung boundary is commonly applied in order to perform a quantitative CT analysis (for example calculating mass and volume), and to classify lung voxels according to their contribution to ventilation. Since the lung boundary near atelectatic or otherwise damaged lung tissue is very delicate and cannot be determined automatically, the segmentation needs to be done manually. This is not only cumbersome, but also error-prone. Most of the segmentation work is performed by medical students who require detailed instructions, and time-consuming inspection is needed to reduce manual errors. Note that this manual process is focused solely on the lung, and no other anatomical structures are considered during the segmentation. Compare Chapter 2 for more details on medical imaging of the lung.

Due to the cumbersome and time-consuming process of manual lung segmentation and the lack of reliable automatic methods (compare Chapter 4.2), the state-of-the-art of three-dimensional thorax models for EIT imaging is limited to the so-called 2.5D models. Only one CT slice at the height of the electrode belt is segmented (thorax boundary, lungs and heart shape, in the most complex cases), and this shape is then extruded vertically. The limitations of these models are discussed in Chapters 3 and 6. Beyond that, these models can be generated in only a few minutes (segmentation, meshing, *GREIT* training). The generation of true 3D models of the whole thorax, especially for patients with severe lung damage, requires a different approach than manual segmentation (time-consuming) or automated algorithms (not reliable, limited scope, not intuitive).

Our approach, presented in this chapter, tackles all three research areas: Quantitative CT analysis, 3D models for EIT imaging, and the development of a semi-automatic segmentation process. Our workflow contains interactive elements such that the user can refine the segmentation result until satisfied, i.e. until it is equivalent to the manual segmentation. It is much faster and can be used with more confidence by medical students, since the errors resulting from manual segmentation can be reduced significantly. Our approach is also specifically designed to create a multi-material segmentation of several thorax structures, and it is generally not restricted to this kind of anatomy.

An overview of the workflow was published as conference posters [136, 137].

Chapter 4.1 defines our research questions and goals for the segmentation workflow. In Chapter 4.2, we summarize related work and differentiate it from our approach. Our proposed workflow is explained in detail in Chapter 4.3, while Chapter 4.4 presents results concerning segmentation quality, capability, run-time, and interaction. Finally, we highlight the significance of our workflow for clinical research in Chapter 4.5 and conclude the chapter with an outlook on future work (Chapter 4.6).

4.1 Research Question and Goal

The most important requirement for our workflow is the generation of a lung segmentation including severe pathologies (like atelectasis and hyperventilated regions), which is also capable of distinguishing them from regions with very similar characteristics outside the lung, such as pleural effusions and pneumothoraces. A single segmentation algorithm is not suitable for clinical use by medical personnel, as we explain in Chapter 4.2. Therefore a workflow is required which also includes pre- and post-processing steps as well as clearly defined interactions. In addition to the clinically useful lung segmentation, we also want to use the results to generate 3D thorax models for EIT. Thus, we require multi-material segmentations, including thorax shape, heart, bones, lungs, pathological lung tissue, blood vessels, electrodes, and possibly other tissues.

In order to use a lung segmentation method for clinical research regarding EIT and qCT, it is also necessary to consider a variety of medical requirements. Since the current manual contouring of the lung boundary takes several hours, throughput and ease of interaction are most important. At the same time, precision of the result is critical, especially for qCT calculations, i.e. the outcome should be identical to the desired manual result. As medical researchers do not trust fully automated, black-box-like algorithms, elaborate interaction mechanisms need to be considered. Also, automated segmentation is not feasible for the large variety of pathological lungs which occur in clinical practice. It is therefore reasonable to include the physician's expert knowledge explicitly into the process. In cases where our method fails to produce a satisfying lung boundary, the user should be able to fall back to the manual contouring. However, its usage should be rather minimal since it is slow and error-prone, especially if performed by inexperienced medical students. To avoid tedious inspection and error correction, the whole process should be transparent and comprehensible such that the medical user has great confidence in the segmentation result.

From these requirements, we define the following goals for our segmentation approach. We want to develop an interactive workflow which is easy to use by medical experts. It should be significantly faster than the current manual process, while manual delineation of the lung boundary in very difficult cases should still be possible. To reduce this tedious work to a minimum, an intuitive, but very effective interaction should be explicitly included by design to incorporate the medical experience of the user. In addition to the lungs, our workflow should allow for multi-material segmentation so that 3D thorax model generation becomes possible. Finally, the results should be the same as for the manual approach, i.e. the workflow needs to be iterative until the user is satisfied.

4.2 Differentiation from Related Work

The first thing to note about thoracic CT segmentation is the lack of integrated multi-purpose frameworks. We are aware of one framework in the literature that, similar to our method, fuses different methods into a well-designed process to extract a variety of information from the pelvic area [77]. Other methods are usually very specialized for a single purpose (such as segmentation of rib cage, heart, lungs, or diaphragm) and are mostly automatic with almost no planned user interaction. We have found through our collaborators that medical experts frequently distrust automatic black-box-like algorithms and that it makes more sense to incorporate expert knowledge explicitly with the use of interactive segmentation. Also, automatic segmentation methods still require profound knowledge of the underlying theory to adjust parameters, which is not feasible for clinicians.

In the following, we present a short review of several methods for thorax segmentation, and show how none of them fulfills our requirements on their own.

There is a vast number of thorax segmentation methods of which we briefly mention a few here. In [143], a segmentation-by-registration approach is introduced that elastically registers a CT scan of a healthy subject to pathological data. The most notable drawbacks of this method are the small slice thickness of 1 mm, which is not yet commonly used in clinical practice, the long computation time of four hours, and the use of a healthy ground truth which only works for patients with similar geometry. Therefore it would be necessary to maintain a variety of normal CT scans for different body geometries (age, gender, weight, height, etc.). This is one of our long-term goals, but not yet feasible in the near future.

The Random Walk introduced by Grady [69] is often successfully used for segmentation. In this approach, the probability is computed that a random walker starting at an unlabeled pixel arrives at each of the seed points. Although very similar to the method we use, the Random Walk cannot handle further iterations with new seed points in a similar efficient and user-friendly manner.

A group of publications make use of the Optimal Surface Segmentation method introduced by Li et al. [99]. Yalamanchili et al. [171] describe an automatic procedure to segment the diaphragm, which is a useful application to find the boundary between thorax and abdomen. However, problems can occur with pathological lungs containing atelectasis and consolidated tissue, or when the heart touches the diaphragm. This can happen frequently in our data since pneumothoraces or bullae tend to shift the heart to unnatural shapes and positions. We believe that user-guided segmentation is more appropriate to reliably separate the diaphragm from the upper thorax.

Hua et al. [86] place their focus on pathological lungs, but their data contains a slice thickness between 0.3 and 0.9 mm, which is not commonly used in clinical practice. In terms of the presented results, it is not completely clear how their method can cope with different pathologies without any user interaction. Generally, a proper cost function design is necessary for each application of the Optimal Surface Segmentation. These cost functions are quite theoretic, and difficult to comprehend or to edit by medical users.

Overall, discrimination of pathological tissue from surrounding healthy tissue is difficult, even for experts (Figure 4.10). For example, to delineate the delicate boundary between non-aerated lung tissue and pleural effusion outside of the lung, a lot of experience is required. Fully automatic algorithms are not able to perform this task accurately and reliably. Some of them also involve a kind of elastic deformation or active contours [89, 31, 151, 133, 141, 150] which are difficult to use in practical applications. Other approaches use image- or shape-based computational methods, but are not applicable to the challenging CT data of patients with severe lung injury [110, 90, 120, 34].

In the following, we present several interactive segmentation approaches that explicitly include user-provided information. Kockelkorn et al. [96] acknowledge the challenges concerned with pathological lungs in terms of automated algorithms. They divide the data set into small volumes of interest with homogeneous texture, calculate texture features, and perform a k-NN classification. The user corrects any misclassified regions. It is reported that segmentation times are as low as ten minutes, since only about 1% of the regions need to be corrected. Unfortunately, the data sets presented in the paper are not as challenging as many of ours. Additionally, the slice thickness is about 1 mm, much smaller than commonly used in clinical practice.

Yang et al. [173] exploit user-drawn foreground/background sketches to interactively segment liver tumors. They apply online learning using the gray-level histogram and SIFT features. On the downside, their method is only used on 2D slices, thus requiring to process each slice individually, and neglecting present 3D information.

Top et al. [156] use Active Learning for interactive 3D segmentation, meaning that training data is automatically selected for the user to label. They calculate a plane of maximal uncertainty from image features, which is presented to the user as a suggestion for additional input. Integrating the Random Walk algorithm, they report a time reduction by two thirds. While being a very interesting approach, the method is only applied to bones and liver, represented by data sets that are not as challenging as our lung data.

A different problem is tackled by Wang and Yushkevich [161]. Multiple labelings of the same region from different experts can deviate significantly. The correlation between the available data is exploited to provide a fused segmentation with high confidence.

Andrews et al. [7] significantly improve the runtime of the original Random Walk algorithm by incorporating offline pre-computations to allow for real-time updates of the segmentation.

Similar to many other approaches, Sofka et al. [144] determine a lung shape model from an annotated database. They automatically calculate several landmarks, such as ribs and spine, from an initialization at the trachea. These landmarks are then used to align the shape model.

As mentioned before, many segmentation methods are only concerned with a single object. Lucas et al. [102] extend Geodesic Active Contours to work with multiple objects.

Liu et al. [101] aim to remedy the dependence of Geodesic Active Contours on strong gradients. They use regional statistical information to ensure the homogeneity of the interior of segmented regions.

Mostly used for segmentation of natural images into foreground and background, segmentation-by-sketching methods are now also used in medicine-related application papers [46, 159]. Karimov et al. [88] attempt to interactively post-process liver segmentations. These particular works implement sketching on 3D volume-rendered data. In clinical practice, however, it is more convenient for the expert to interact with 2D images.

We therefore rely on a sketching approach introduced by Bai and Sapiro [11]. The geodesic distance between pixels is used as a weighting function, taking into account the physical distance between a pixel and a sketch, weighted with statistical properties acquired from kernel density estimation. A voxel receives the label of a certain sketch if the probability density along the shortest path through the volume does not vary strongly. This method easily scales to 3D data, uses fast computation methods, and has the very promising feature of fusing the actual distance of pixels with statistical properties learned from the sketches. If the result of one iteration is not satisfying, additional sketches can easily be added until the segmentation is complete (see Chapter 4.3 for more details on this method).

We would like to point out that the segmentation workflow we present in the next section does not include any novel algorithms. We concluded from the literature that there are so many segmentation algorithms which do not solve our particular task. This task comprises the generation of a multi-material, three-dimensional thorax segmentation from very challenging data. Our method is supposed to be interactively operated by a medical expert, thus usability and understandability needs to be tuned to this particular group of users. Our workflow requires the possibility for the expert to modify the result in a convenient, fast and interactive way until satisfied. Finally, input and output data need to be seamlessly integrated into the practical workflow of the expert.

With these requirements in mind, it is apparent why isolated algorithms do not suffice for our task. The methods as presented in the literature are neither easily usable nor comprehensible to most medical experts because they require a profound mathematical and computational knowledge. This cannot be demanded from a medical expert. The same applies to parameter choices and tuning. Many user studies evaluating a particular interactive visualization or image processing technique report that most users were overburdened by the parameter selection and stayed with the default settings. We therefore aim to develop a complete workflow with a sophisticated and powerful algorithm at its core. The workflow is supposed to abstract from the algorithmic and mathematical details, and to provide empirically chosen parameters that are known to work well for the task at hand. User interactions should be constrained to a small set of actions that do not need to be tediously learned by the medical expert. Some best practices or heuristics should be presented to the user without requiring detailed knowledge of the underlying algorithms. Finally, many important smaller tasks need to be included in the workflow, such as the removal of distracting image parts, and post-processing steps in an interactive feedback loop.

4.3 Proposed Segmentation Workflow

Data and Challenges

We use thoracic CT data with an in-slice resolution of 512×512 pixels (ca. 0.6 mm per pixel) and a slice thickness of $3-5$ mm, resulting in 35-100 slices in general. The gray values represent Hounsfield Units (HU), where -1024 HU is defined as air, and 0 HU as water. High-density material like metal is capped at 2976 HU, resulting in a gray value range of 4000 HU.

CT image data, although providing a high anatomical resolution, are considered to be generally noisy and artifact-prone. Most severe artifacts are caused by high-density materials like bones and metal objects (e.g. monitoring equipment, electrodes, or heart catheters). These artifacts include streaking, dark bands, and partial volume effects. Furthermore, slice thickness in clinical data is typically about $3-5$ mm (compared to $0.1-1$ mm used in several research papers), while the pixel width is about 0.6 mm. These anisotropic characteristics introduce several problems for 3D image processing. Confer Chapter 2.1 for more details on clinical CT imagery.

Thorax segmentation of healthy patients is quite straight-forward, for example by histogram-based thresholding. However, many EIT patients suffer from severe lung damage, such as atelectasis, opacification, gasless lung tissue, pleural effusion (which is difficult to distinguish from surrounding tissue), and pneumothoraces, which to automatic image processing methods often appear similar to aerated lung tissue. See Figures 2.1 and 2.2 for examples of healthy and pathological lung slices from humans and pigs.

Since EIT model generation and especially quantitative analysis of the lung require a precise segmentation of the lung boundary, the pathological lung regions are of critical interest. At the same time, fully automated segmentation methods fail to produce reliable results on such data.

The most important requirement for clinical use is timely availability and throughput. When a patient suffering from severe pulmonary damage arrives in the emergency room, a radiologist visually inspects the full-body CT scan using 2D slices to decide further actions. This commonly takes several minutes. To obtain additional quantitative information from the CT data or to generate an EIT model, segmentation of the lung is necessary during inspection (confer for example [131]). In case of manual segmentation, which is the most common method in clinical research, the whole lung boundary is delineated, including non-aerated tissue. With our approach, an explicit mask will be computed for this kind of tissue, making quantitative calculations easier. To profit from the physician's expert knowledge, the process needs to be highly usable and interactive, while the incorporated methods and algorithms should also be comprehensible.

Workflow Methodology

Our proposed workflow is outlined in Figure 4.1, where green frames indicate phases of required user interaction.

We roughly divide the intensity range into five materials:

- M_N (Noise and air): Low-density noise like streaking artifacts and dark band effects caused by metal objects. This range also includes air, hyperinflated lung tissue, pneumothoraces, and emphysema.

- M_L (Lung tissue): Aerated lung tissue is easy to identify, but this also includes atelectatic, consolidated, or collapsed lung sections, where the HU values are very similar to M_T.

- M_T (Thorax tissue): Muscle, fat, blood, and also pleural effusions inside the pleural space, but outside the lung.

- M_B (Bone tissue): Bones can be easily segmented, but due to interpolation artifacts, bone-like voxels also appear on high-density material transitions. They can also be confused with contrast agents.

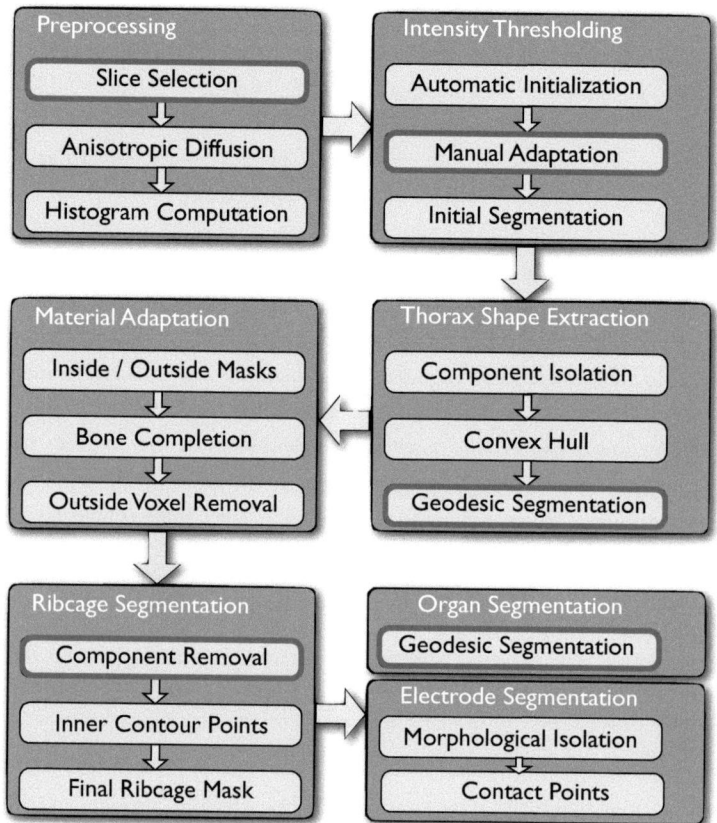

Figure 4.1: A visual overview of our segmentation workflow with intended user intactions highlighted in green.

- M_M (Metal): This involves the upper end of the density spectrum, but also overlaps with the range of bone voxels.

Confer Figure 4.2 for a sample histogram.

In contrast to most other segmentation algorithms which only work on a binary mask for a single structure of interest, we are able to produce a multi-material segmentation of human and pig thorax data. The delineation and especially separation of healthy and pathological lung tissue is a major benefit

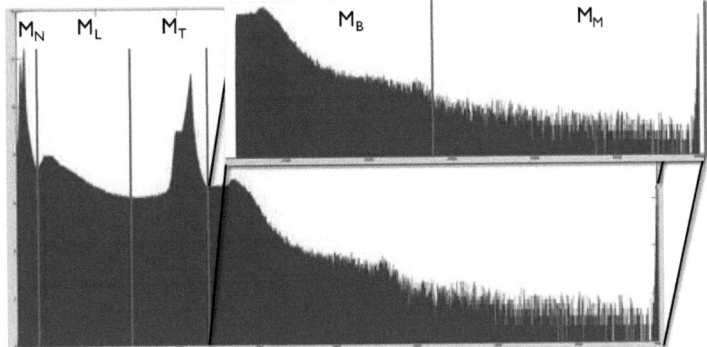

Figure 4.2: Hounsfield scale log-histogram of the thorax with typical material boundaries marked in red.

for clinical research by itself, but we also include other tissues for the EIT model as well.

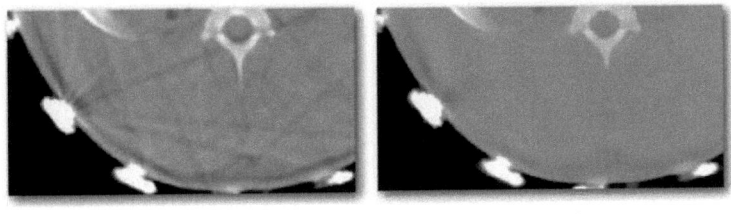

(a) Severe artifacts before smoothing. (b) After anisotropic smoothing.

Figure 4.3: Anisotropic filtering to smooth image noise while preserving edge locations.

Our workflow starts with the presentation of the CT slices. The user can scroll through the data with a slider, and select the start and end slices of the volume of interest, containing the lung. By restricting the data set to this subvolume, we reduce computation times and segmentation errors. Metal-induced artifacts severely influence data quality. In fact, streaks, dark bands, and partial volume effects make an initialization by thresholding very difficult. We therefore apply a 3D anisotropic diffusion filter [116] to smooth homogeneous areas while preserving strong edges and their location. Parameters are empirically chosen so no user interaction is necessary. Edge preservation is important because for most of the remaining steps, we will use the non-filtered data. This is necessary since weak edges, such as the transition between pathological lung and surrounding tissue, are removed during smoothing, but are critical for the segmentation, compare Figure 4.3. The log-histogram of the smoothed data reveals several peaks corresponding to different tissues (see Figures 4.2 and 7.4). An initial segmentation is determined based on standard empirical ranges, but the user can also tune the boundaries to the actual data interactively, as demonstrated in Figure 4.4.

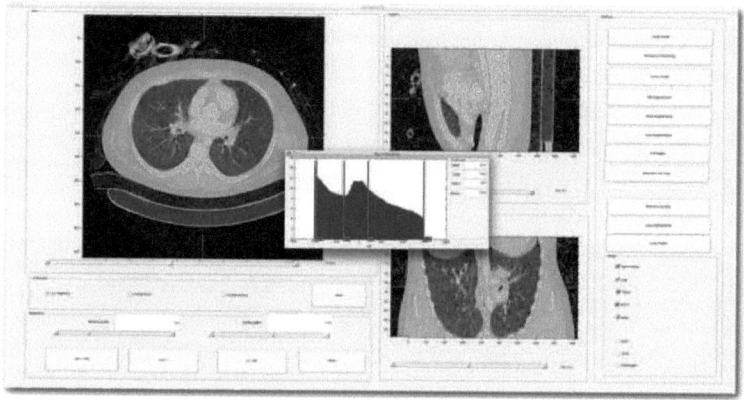

Figure 4.4: Screenshot of our GUI for initialization of the segmentation using Hounsfield scale thresholds.

Thorax shape is very important for Electrical Impedance Tomography [20, 3, 114, 21, 74, 22, 73, 154] but it also allows to remove voxels outside the thorax which otherwise would confuse automatic methods.

We use the binary mask for the soft tissue M_T from the previous step and apply several morphological image filters: A majority filter removes isolated small groups of pixels. An erosion filter removes thin connections of otherwise separated components. Finally, the majority filter is applied again to remove components that became isolated during the erosion.

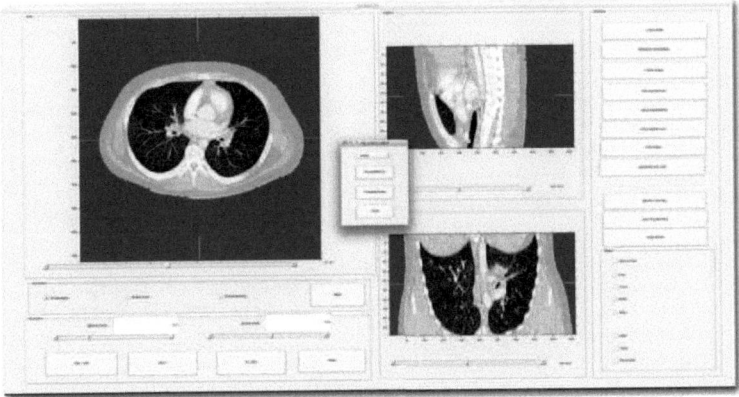

Figure 4.5: Screenshot of our GUI displaying a successful thorax shape separation from spurious image elements.

Since small, isolated structures and very thin connections between larger structures are now eliminated, we apply the Connected Component Analysis (CCA, [48]) and then perform thresholding by area using an empirical value which can also be adapted manually. The result will contain a single component corresponding to the thorax. Thorax shape is extracted from the boundaries of this component in each slice. In case some spurious objects like medical equipment were included in this component, the user can remove these objects interactively using our sketching approach (see below). A result is depicted in Figure 4.5.

The initial segmentation is then updated with the new knowledge using inside/outside masks. Lung, thorax, and low-density voxels outside the thorax are removed and low-density voxels inside the thorax are kept since they either contribute to hyper-inflated lung areas and pneumothoraces or are caused by dark band artifacts - a distinction which we leave to the medical user.

In the next step, the volume enclosed by the ribcage is isolated since important structures like aerated and pathological lung tissue, heart, and aorta are located there. An example for rib cage extraction is given by Condurache et al. [35], but we prefer a more stable approach. As with the thorax shape extraction, the user manually removes objects that touch the ribs due to par-

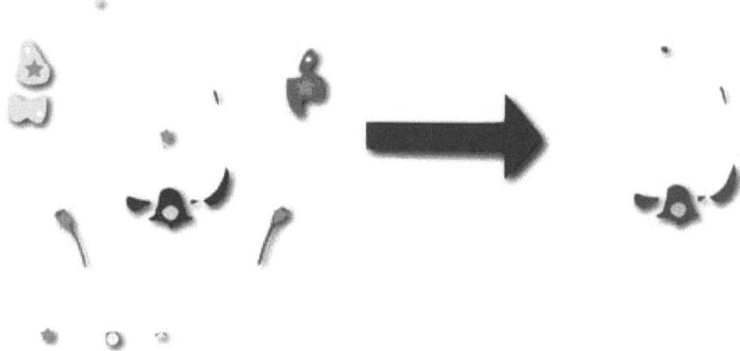

Figure 4.6: Procedure to remove high-density objects not contributing to the ribcage in 3D from 2D user input (green stars).

tial volume effects, such as heart catheters or drainages for pneumothorax treatment. Using again the three-dimensional CCA, a spurious object that does not contribute to the rib cage is removed by a single click in one slice. Figure 4.6 shows a result of such interaction. Blue shapes contribute to the rib cage, while the others are different bones or metal objects. Green stars indicate mouse clicks that select the objects for removal, which is executed in 3D. Thus, only very few slices need to be manually processed by the user.

The inner boundary of the ribs and spine is then computed from the individual contours. This is depicted in Figure 4.7(a). The green points are those rib contour points that face toward the center of the convex hull (red polygon, blue circle). Obviously, not the whole region inside the rib-cage is captured. Therefore, the shape is augmented with the initial lung mask to enclose the whole ribcage and lung. We can now restrict the rest of the segmentation process to this volume of interest (Figure 4.7(b)).

An alternative, more sophisticated approach involving 3D deformable models is reported by Ding et al. [49], which we might integrate in the future. Also, Gargouri et al. [64] present an explicit rib cage segmentation which might result in a more robust and precise enclosing of the volume of interest.

The geodesic segmentation method by Bai and Sapiro [11] distinguishes between foreground, background, and neutral voxels. The first two can be

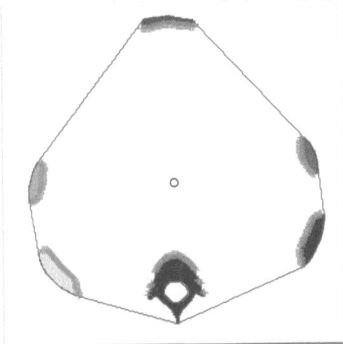 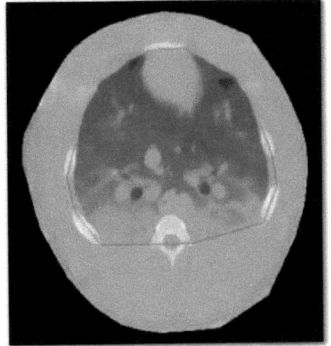

(a) Green points mark inward pointing rib contour points.

(b) The final mask including lung tissue (green) and the ribcage shape (blue).

Figure 4.7: Extraction of the volume inside the ribcage.

determined by drawing sketches into regions of interest in selected slices of the CT data set, as shown in Figure 4.8(a). While the sketching is only performed in 2D slices, the segmentation is conducted in 3D. The shortest path between each voxel and all sketches is computed with the restriction that the probability density function along the path should have a minimal gradient. In contrast to similar approaches, statistical properties of regions of interest as well as the spatial distances between voxels and sketches are seamlessly integrated into the computation.

Note that the original approach works on color images with the *Lab* color representation as feature vectors. Our results using only the gray values of the CT images were not satisfying. Therefore, we used several features from ultrasound texture discrimination [112], which have also been applied to object tracking in noisy and low-quality images that lack distinctive gradients [135]. These include gradient strength, difference from mean, and horizontal and vertical residuals in addition to the original gray values.

To increase the number of pre-classified voxels from the sketches, we extended the interaction to free-hand closed curves. They do not take longer to draw than single sketches, but capture a multiple of the voxels. As a best practice for sketch placement, we experienced that removing over-segmented

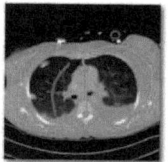 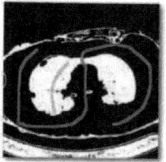 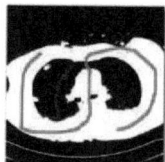 

(a) Foreground (blue) and background sketches (red) to segment the lung.

(b) Probability field for voxels belonging to foreground.

(c) Probability field for voxels belonging to background.

(d) Geodesic distances for foreground from small (blue) to large (red).

Figure 4.8: Sketch-based segmentation following Bai and Sapiro [11].

regions by additional background sketches is quite cumbersome and unnecessary work for the user. We think that a good policy is to start with very few sketches, run the segmentation, and then draw additional foreground sketches in under-segmented regions. Due to the fast computation of the geodesic segmentation, this is feasible and provides a very intuitive interaction.

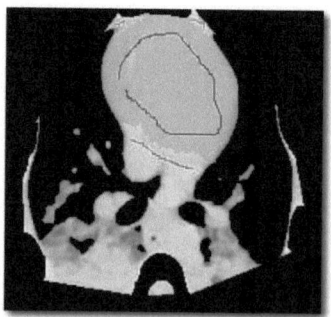 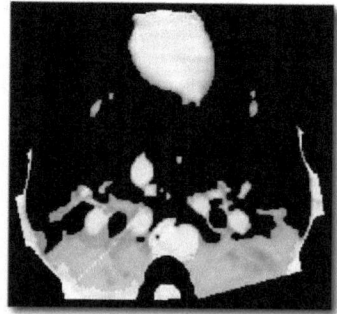

(a) Heart segmentation from four sketches.

(b) Segmentation of atelectasis (green) without blood vessels (circular objects).

Figure 4.9: Examples of successful segmentations inside the ribcage.

Similar to almost all presented segmentation methods, this sketching approach only provides a single material segmentation by classifying each voxel as either foreground or background. Fortunately, the structures of interest in our data can be handled sequentially, thereby feeding already known classifications as prior information to the algorithm. For example, all voxels outside the rib cage are not of interest for lung and heart segmentation. Therefore, these voxels are initially labeled as background. This increases prior information significantly.

The heart is the largest non-lung structure inside the rib cage. It is connected to the thoracic wall and to the major blood vessels, and sometimes touches the diaphragm. Lung injuries like pneumothoraces or bullae can shift the heart's shape and position, making methods based on shape models difficult to use. We draw sketches inside the heart and also place background sketches on undesired structures and components that touch the heart, like the ascending aorta; see Figure 4.9(a). The geodesic segmentation produces very satisfying results from sketches in just a few slices, since we only require the general shape of the heart, not its precise sections.

The procedure is repeated for the descending aorta and for atelectatic or otherwise poorly aerated lung tissue (Figure 4.9(b)). After each segmentation step, the obtained mask is added to the background mask to further increase the number of voxels that are known not to belong to the current object of interest.

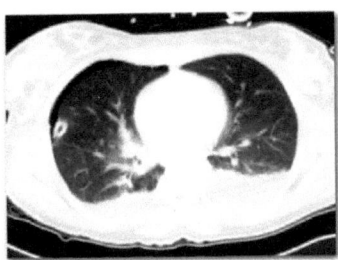
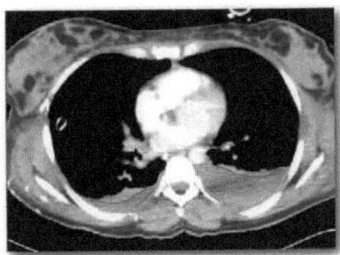

(a) A pneumothorax (black) can be seen in the top left lung region.

(b) The dorsal lung boundary (blue) compared to the boundary of the pleural space (orange) in the presence of pleural effusion.

Figure 4.10: Different windows on the Hounsfield scale to visually assess the lung boundary.

One of the most important practical observations during the collaboration

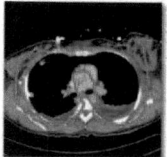 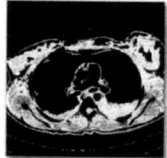 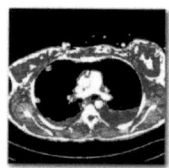 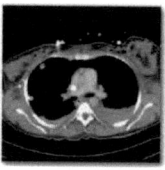

(a) Foreground (blue) and background sketches (red).   (b) Probability field for voxels belonging to foreground.   (c) Probability field for voxels belonging to background.   (d) Final segmentation (green).

Figure 4.11: Segmentation example of atelectasis with three sketches.

with our medical partners was that they are able to separate the pathological lung tissue from surrounding tissue by noting the small intensity changes and weak boundaries (see Figure 4.10). This information is either assessed only visually, or quantified by tedious manual segmentation. We incorporate this expert knowledge into our approach by sketching, which is fast and intuitive to use for the expert. It also provides a good initialization of the statistical models for different tissues, enabling the automatic segmentation step to complete tedious work of accurately tracing the boundaries. This becomes feasible due to the difference between the statistical distributions of the different tissues, which are only accessible with the prior information from the user-provided sketches, as shown in Figure 4.11(c)-(d) and Figure 4.14(b).

Figure 4.12 details how the user interaction to segment pathological lung tissue works. Black regions are determined to be background from prior steps. Here, space outside the thorax as well as the ribs and healthy lung tissue are already segmented. From the rib cage extraction, we can constrain the input volume even further. Two blue sketches inside the pathological tissue serve as foreground markers. Three red sketches exclude adjacent structures of similar appearance, here the descending aorta and soft tissue between the ribs. Note that the segmentation process is performed in 3D, thus sketches are not necessary in all slices. The green shape highlights the resulting segmentation.

Since our pig data was recorded during animal studies with combined CT and EIT images, we have the opportunity to locate the electrode positions explicitly instead of being forced to model them by some other means. Knowing

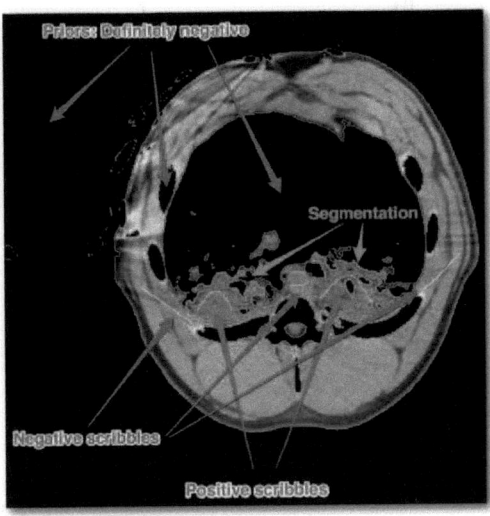

Figure 4.12: Example of segmentation by sketching, highlighting prior information and user-drawn sketches.

the electrode plane, its angle towards the transverse plane, and the exact position on the skin is very crucial for EIT image reconstruction and helps to significantly reduce artifacts [21].

The first challenge is to remove all metal objects from the mask M_M that are not one of the 16 electrodes, such as the adapter connecting the EIT device with the electrode belt, and other medical equipment. Due to actual contact or partial volume effects, these structures can touch the electrodes. Our solution allows for a fast and convenient removal of these elements, as shown in Figure 4.13(b). All metal objects near the thorax boundary are projected into a plane. Due to their rectangular shape, the electrodes are clearly visible on the projection. The user then draws a polygon enclosing all electrodes, which is shown here in blue. With this single interaction, the electrodes can be properly separated from other objects in 3D. Due to the metal-induced artifacts, it is not possible to recover the exact electrode shape. Figure 4.13(a) depicts typical challenges, such as streaks (blue arrow), and partial volume effects of low-density voxels (red arrow) and high-density voxels (purple line). Thus,

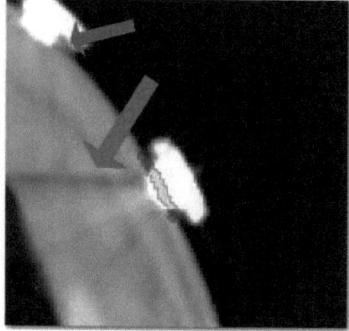 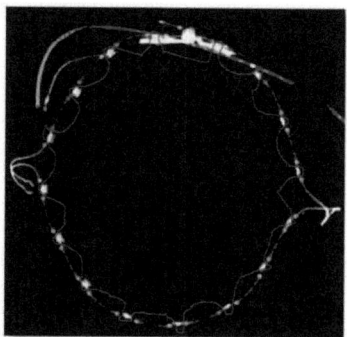

(a) Streaking (blue arrow) and partial volume effects (red arrow and purple line) near the electrode/thorax contact.

(b) User-drawn polygon (blue) to separate electrodes and other metal objects.

Figure 4.13: Electrode segmentation challenges.

we only compute the contact location of each electrode with the skin in each slice. First, the centroid of each electrode shape is determined as well as the centroid of all electrode voxels. We then intersect the line between each electrode's centroid and the total centroid with the thorax shape. This results in the contact locations. From the boundary contour we also compute the skin normal to obtain the orientation of the electrode with respect to the thorax. The precise electrode shape cannot be recovered due to the severe metal-induced artifacts, but it is known from the manufacturer. We therefore reconstruct the electrode shapes from the positions and orientations such that they touch the thorax in each slice. Confer Figure 5.2(a) in Chapter 5 for results of the electrode segmentation.

The output of the whole workflow is a multi-material volume mask containing the segmentation.

Details on the Core Segmentation Algorithm

As shortly described above, the core segmentation method of our workflow is the sketch-based geodesic algorithm by Bai and Sapiro [11]. It features three central elements that are detailed in this section. The first element is the fusion of image features and statistical information gathered from user-provided background/foreground sketches. Second, voxels are classified by computing the shortest path towards the sketches, which extends naturally to 3D. Finally, a convenient and efficient method to update the segmentation interactively by adding sketches is provided.

The algorithm is very flexible in terms of possible image features. Since the authors' interest lies in natural images, they use the *Lab* color vector, but many other features are possible, as we have shortly mentioned before. We will follow the algorithm using an artificial example, as shown in Figure 4.8. Since the aerated lung can easily be classified automatically, this is not a real-world use case, but it provides a visual guide for the algorithmic details. The blue sketch indicates lung tissue (foreground), while the red one contains several background structures, such as soft tissue, bones, and the heart. From these user-drawn sketches (also referred to as scribbles), the probability density both for foreground and background is computed for each feature using a kernel density estimation. These densities are visualized in Figure 4.14(a), with the lung on the left (low-density values), and the background on the right. Note that for this example, there is almost no overlap between the densities due to the very different tissue characteristics. In practice however, the densities usually overlap significantly (compare Figure 4.14(b)).

Following the notation in the paper, let $\Omega_\mathcal{F}$ be the foreground set with label $\mathcal{F}$, and accordingly $\Omega_\mathcal{B}$ for the background. When $\Pr(\vec{c_x}|\mathcal{F})$ is the probability density value of the foreground for voxel x with feature vector $\vec{c_x}$, then the probability that x belongs to the foreground is

$$P_\mathcal{F} = \frac{\Pr(\vec{c_x}|\mathcal{F})}{\Pr(\vec{c_x}|\mathcal{F}) + \Pr(\vec{c_x}|\mathcal{B})}. \tag{4.1}$$

For our example slice, these values are visualized in Figure 4.8(b) for the foreground, and Figure 4.8(c) for the background. Note that the images are almost binary, indicating that each voxel has a likelihood of close to one to belong to one set only. Figure 4.11 illustrates a more challenging example for the pathological lung, together with the corresponding probability density functions in Figure 4.14(b).

The mathematical details of the geodesic distance computation are very nicely presented in Section 3.1.2 of [11]. In short, each voxel is labeled accord-

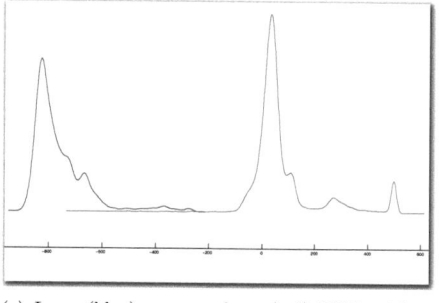 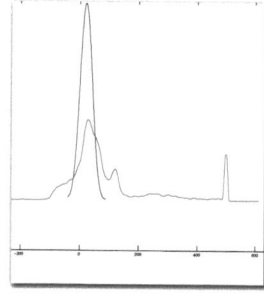

(a) Lung (blue) vs. non-lung (red) PDFs without overlap.

(b) Atelectasis (blue) vs. other tissue (red) with significant overlap.

Figure 4.14: Probability densitiy functions (PDF) for segmentation by sketching.

ing to the shortest geodesic distance to a sketch. This distance is weighted with $W(x) = \nabla P_{\mathcal{F}}(x)$ for the foreground, i.e. a path's length not only depends on the actual spatial distance, but also on the probability density field. This lets paths through homogeneous regions with low variance of the probabilities become much shorter than paths that cross regions of varying probability. In our example, the geodesic distance of all voxels to the blue foreground sketch is visualized in Figure 4.8(d). The aerated lung close to the sketch is assigned very low distances (indicated by blue colors), while the distance for the right lung increases significantly. This is not surprising since the shortest paths for these voxels have to cross a background sketch at the mediastinum. For everything outside the lungs, the distance essentially becomes infinite (red). The final result for a voxel is then the lowest distance to either a foreground or a background sketch. In our case, this would result in a segmentation of the whole aerated lung, although only the left side was sketched. The result can easily be constrained by thresholding the distance field. In almost all of our test cases, distances for regions that are not intended to contribute to the segmentation grow very fast.

Although only a few sketches in only a few slices are necessary for a sufficient 3D segmentation, the first iteration is sometimes not satisfying. The algorithm by Bai and Sapiro provides a very convenient way to add both foreground and background sketches, and to then update the segmentation efficiently. Also, changes to the result are constrained locally.

As mentioned before, we integrated several image features into the algorithm. As we have no color information available, the gray values alone do not suffice to properly separate the challenging regions. Often, gradient information is used, but this is also not enough due to the noisy nature of the CT data and the general low-edge structures that are of our interest. Since the method allows for a large variety of features, we are able to use texture-based features as described above, which deliver satisfactory results.

Implementation

We implemented a first functional prototype using Matlab. As detailed below, it is very slow and shows great potential for optimization. With a sophisticated implementation exploiting parallelization, especially on the GPU, we are confident to achieve almost real-time results. Confer our future plans in Chapter 7.3. In the meantime, this prototype successfully demonstrates the capability of our workflow in principle.

Several GUI elements are integrated in our workflow. First, the user is provided with a scrollable slice view to briefly inspect the data set and select the first and last slice containing lung tissue. In the presence of pathology, this is a non-trivial task for automatic methods. In addition, the user places a single mouse click inside the trachea for future use in airway segmentation (compare [19]) or shape model initialization [144].

As shown in Figure 4.4, a histogram-based thresholding is then performed interactively. The GUI is initialized with standard values for material boundaries, and the resulting segmentation is displayed on top of each orthogonal view of the data set. The user can then manually modify the thresholds with real-time updates in the visualization. This can be done by dragging the red bars inside the histogram, or by explicitly entering the Hounsfield values. In our example, it is apparent that several blood vessels are classified as bone material (red) due to a contrast agent. The user can now try to raise the bone threshold to constrain the mask to the actual bones. The real-time update indicates whether this is successful, or whether post-processing is necessary in a future step due to a histogram overlap.

Sketches for the geodesic segmentation or the component removal (see below) can be drawn in any view. Figure 4.5 shows a successful thorax shape extraction by removing all touching external components such as medical equipment with very few user interactions. The type of sketch can be selected from the popup dialog box, here in the middle of the screen. There are two options for sketches. The first is a simple scribble with a user-specified width, see for example the red background scribbles for heart segmentation in Figure 4.9(a). In the same figure, the blue foreground sketch inside the heart encloses a polygonal region, capturing several magnitudes more voxels than a scribble, while hardly any extra time is required from the user. This allows for a better statistical model of the foreground and background distributions, which is actually necessary for challenging tasks such as pathology segmentation (compare Figures 4.9(b), 4.10(b), 4.12, 4.11, and 4.14(b)).

Especially in the cases of thorax shape and rib cage extraction, some components may touch each other, for example by partial volume effects. In order to separate them, we draw rough scribbles which remove the marked pixels, creating a gap between the objects. In the next step, all connected components are calculated in 3D, and a slice-based visualization is presented to the user, as shown in Figure 4.6. Each component is color-coded consistently through all slices. Thus, the user can simply select a 3D component for removal by clicking it in a single slice (green stars). This unique challenge has never been considered in the whole literature on medical image segmentation, but occurs quite frequently in real-world patient data.

Most of the geodesic segmentation is straight forward to implement, such as the feature computation (gradient strength, difference to mean, gray values, and residues in each volume direction, compare [135]), kernel density estimation for the probability density functions, evaluation of these functions for each voxel, and conversion of the foreground/background shapes to individual voxel sets. The geodesic shortest path computation using Fast Marching is based on a Matlab implementation by Kroon, called Multistencil Fast Marching Method[1], which exploits optimization methods published by Hassouna and

---

[1] http://www.mathworks.com/matlabcentral/fileexchange/
24531-accurate-fast-marching

Faraq [82] and Bærentzen [9] to achieve linear runtime. In order to further reduce the computational effort, we constrain the volume of interest to a region near the scribbles because segmentation quality decreases for remote regions. We formulated the best practice policy to start with very few sketches, and then iterate by adding further sketches. This is more convenient and effective than tediously trying to correct over-segmentation and leaking. As suggested by Bai and Sapiro, we compute the distances separately for each feature, and then average the result.

In conclusion, the very efficient algorithms used for this workflow have great potential for parallelization and other optimizations. We are thus confident to achieve almost real-time results in the near future.

Limitations

As noted before, one of the most severe limitations as of now is the inefficient implementation of our prototype. The runtime is far from interactive, taking more than 40 minutes to segment a challenging thorax data set. This is far superior compared to the six hours required for manual segmentation (confer [130]), but not satisfactory for our tasks. However, just measuring the time necessary for interaction resulted in less than 15 minutes. This means that once we can achieve almost real-time computations by optimization, we will meet our goal required for clinical use.

In addition, the usability of interactive workflow steps needs further improvement since they are not very accessible to medical experts at the moment. We will develop a suitable interface in close collaboration with our medical partners in the near future. In general, medical users will require a short training to perform all segmentation steps presented in this workflow. Especially the optimal placement of sketches to minimize the number of iterations during the geodesic segmentation needs some basic understanding of how the algorithm works. Fortunately, a high-level explanation is readily available for this method, and no detailed algorithmic knowledge is required to learn optimal sketch drawing.

4.4 Results

In this section, we present segmentation results from both pigs and human patients. On a smaller scale, Figure 4.9 demonstrates the capability of the sketch-based geodesic segmentation algorithm at the core of our workflow. To the left, the heart is shown with four scribbles. To the right, atelectatic lung tissue is successfully segmented, leaving out blood vessels, despite their similar appearance.

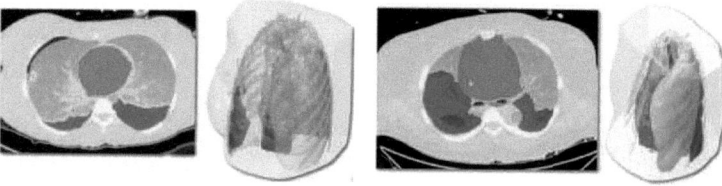

(a) Female human patient with a pneumothorax (blue).

(b) Obese human patient with severe atelectasis (purple).

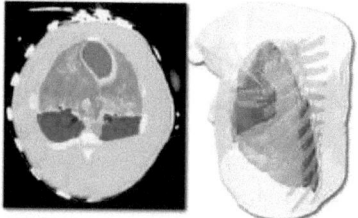

(c) Pig with electrode belt and dorsal lung injury (purple).

Figure 4.15: Segmentation results from our workflow. Yellow: lung, red: heart, green: aorta, blue: air, purple: atelectasis.

Figure 4.15 depicts three thorax data sets, where a single slice, augmented with the segmentation mask is hown on the left, and a 3D visualization of all materials on the right. In Figure 4.15(a), a female patient with a small pneumothorax (blue) and severe pleural effusions outside the lung (purple) is presented. Aerated lung tissue is indicated by yellow, while the heart (red), descending aorta (green), and the rib cage (white) are also shown. Using the same color-coding, Figure 4.15(b) depicts an obese male patient with a significantly enlarged heart and severe atelectasis (purple). Finally, a pig from our collaborators' animal experiments is presented in Figure 4.15(c), where the EIT electrodes are visible as bright structures on the thorax surface, and an induced lung injury is shown in purple.

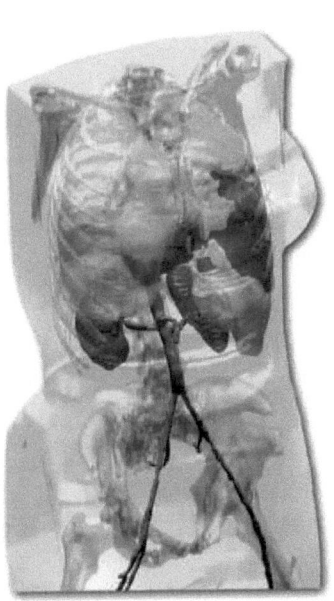

(a) Female patient from Figure 4.15(a). Kidneys are colored in purple and major blood vessels in magenta.

(b) Female patient with additional muscle and brain segmentation.

Figure 4.16: Full body segmentations. CT data for (b) taken from OsiriX.

Although our workflow is specifically designed for multi-material segmentations of the thorax, with a focus on the lungs and their pathologies, we also demonstrate the general applicability to more use cases in Figure 4.16. We segmented full-body CT scans from two female patients. Figure 4.16(a) shows the same patient as Figure 4.15(a) with the pneumothorax (blue) and pleural effusion (purple, in the background). In addition, kidneys (dark purple), liver (orange), skeleton (white), and major blood vessels (magenta) are shown. For the data set to the right[2], we also segmented the muscles (light red) and the brain (white). Compared to manual segmentation, which would have taken several days per data set, we are able to achieve these results in just a few hours, even with our slow and inefficient implementation.

4.5 Significance for Clinical Research

We outlined the many limitations of current segmentation algorithms regarding application in clinical research and practice. We detailed on which kind of solution is required for such usage, and proposed a segmentation workflow to tackle this problem. It was demonstrated that our workflow delivers satisfactory results in terms of segmentation quality, and the methods used have the potential for almost real-time performance. Our solution is virtually unique in that it provides a convenient and interactive means to produce multi-material segmentations of challenging real-world data.

Our medical collaborators look forward to the possibilities that open up once thorax segmentation is not such a time-consuming task anymore. As we describe in Chapter 7, our first collaborative clinical research projects enable a much faster generation of results and allow for more experimentation. It has to be noted, however, that our potential users are somewhat skeptical regarding the usability of our tool. Therefore, we will develop a practical system in close collaboration with them, which is highly usable and easy to learn by medical personnel.

As there is a significant lack of segmentation tools that are usable in clinical research (with a few exceptions mentioned in Chapter 7.3), we plan to publish our software as open source. In addition, our workflow is not limited to thorax and lung segmentation as demonstrated, but can easily be adapted and applied to other organs and tissues as well. Thus, many clinical research groups might benefit from our tool.

---

[2]http://www.osirix-viewer.com/datasets/

4.6 Outlook

As we will complete a fast and usable implementation of our workflow in the near future, we plan a profound evaluation regarding segmentation quality and execution time. We have a large database of pre-segmented lung data from both humans and pigs available to compare our results and those of other algorithms to the gold standard of manual segmentation. In the current setting, clinicians have a choice between fully manual tracing of the lung boundary, and a pre-processing step using Region Growing. For this, a single seed point inside the lung is selected, and the automatically computed lung boundary can be refined afterwards. This works well for healthy lungs in general and for aerated lung parts in patients with lung damage. For the atelectatic tissue, pneumothoraces, and other pathologies, full manual tracing is necessary. To compare this process to our proposed workflow, the manually segmented data sets will be processed again by medical experts familiar with slice-based manual segmentation. Time to completion, number of interaction steps and location error of the resulting lung polygon in each slice will be measured. Of course, processing time is much more important than location error since a manual post-processing is always possible after completing the workflow. The number of interaction steps is crucial for our goal of minimizing user input, and varies for the different types of lung damage. In addition to the lung segmentation, our workflow will provide several more materials such as thorax and heart shape during the process with very little additional overhead.

Apart from the implementation plans, there are two areas where we intend to improve our workflow. First, we will investigate other means than anisotropic filtering for noise reduction, such as Bilateral Filtering, published by Tomasi and Manduchi [155]. Another promising approach from 3D ultrasound filtering is to perform a lowest-variance streamline integration, resulting in a structure-preserving filter response (compare [148]).

As most CT artifacts and noise are caused by high-density objects such as metal, we plan to include an explicit artifact reduction method. An example of early works is presented by Wei et al. [163], while Chen et al. [32] apply the so-called in-painting technique by Criminisi et al. [39]. This method shows great potential for metal artifact reduction with limited user interaction, but a potential drawback is the need to perform a backward and forward projection of the CT data without knowing the exact parameters from the device manufacturer.

Chapter 5

Three-dimensional EIT Models

In order to generate 3D thorax models for EIT imaging, a tetrahedral Finite Element (FEM) mesh needs to be constructed from the volumetric multi-material segmentation presented in Chapter 4. Certain requirements make it necessary to develop a specifically tailored meshing solution. First, the mesh density around the electrodes (which are modeled based on the Complete Electrode Model, CEM, see Chapter 2) is required to be very large. This is due to the large sensitivity of the electric field near the electrodes. Additionally, the mesh density needs to be large at material transitions. Note that multi-material FEM meshes are not too common in the literature and in practice. To reduce mesh complexity, size, and processing, internal, homogeneous structures should be as sparse as possible in terms of tetrahedra count. Finally, a high amount of automation in the workflow is needed to allow a good integration into clinical processes.

Parts of the results from this chapter are published as a conference abstract [139] and a paper [138].

Chapter 5.1 details post-processing steps of the segmentation and the meshing workflow using the software *BioMesh 3D*. In Chapter 5.2, we show how the *BioMesh 3D* output is transformed to an *EIDORS*-compatible forward model. The modeling of a conductivity distribution as well as the generation of *GREIT*-based inverse models is also detailed. In Chapter 5.3 we present results of our model generation workflow and compare them to state-of-the-art 2.5D models, as reported by Salz et al. [138]. Finally, we provide an outlook on future work in Chapter 5.4.

5.1 Generation of Finite Element Models from the Segmentation

Post-processing of the Volumetric Segmentation

Although the *EIDORS* software uses *netgen* as a meshing solution for 2D and 2.5D models, this is not suitable for 3D models as well as for complex 2.5D models (confer Chapter 3.2). Our collaborators from the SCI Institute in Salt Lake City, USA, use their own software *BioMesh 3D*, which is included into their problem solving environment *SCIRun* [1]. They perform not only meshing of complex anatomical models, but also simulations of bio-electrical properties as well as high-quality visualizations. More details on *BioMesh 3D* are presented in the next section; here, only the post-processing steps are shown which are necessary to make our multi-material segmentations suitable as input to *BioMesh 3D*.

In contrast to the work on bio-electrical modeling and simulation, for example by Schmidt et al. [140], Burton et al. [28], Dannhauer et al. [42], McDowell et al. [107] and Wang et al. [160], precision of our models up to millimeters is not as important, since EIT images generally have a low resolution. Furthermore, access to workstations with large amounts of RAM (i.e. more than 32 GB) is not given in clinical research, and computation times are strongly increased for very detailed models. Thus, we resample our 512×512 CT slices to 256×256 pixels to constrain the size and complexity of the final mesh.

The first phase of *BioMesh 3D* isolates the materials and writes them into their own NRRD files. Afterwards, each material is smoothed by limiting the curvature (a process called tightening) as proposed by Williams and Rossignac [166], to deal with stepping artifacts from the slice thickness and other unwanted rough structures. Then, a boundary surface is computed for each material using an isosurface algorithm.

Meshing with BioMesh 3D

BioMesh 3D executes several phases. Each of them writes extensive output to a file, such that all phases can be executed or processed at different times. It produces multi-material, adaptive meshes of high-quality. However, it is completely CPU-based, slow, and sometimes convergence to a final mesh is not even successful. The first two phases are concerned with pre-processing of the input segmentation, as explained above.

Afterwards, a medial axis is computed using a point cloud based iterative process. After locating material junctions, seed-points for a particle system are randomly placed onto these junctions. A sizing field based on the distance of a boundary surface to the medial axis serves as an energy metric, where the particles move to state of minimal energy while remaining on the boundary surface of their material. The meshing software *Tetgen*[1] produces a tetrahedral mesh from surfaces that share nodes of the final particle system. *Tetgen* is a widely used meshing software based on Delaunay tetrahedralization.

BioMesh 3D uses structured text files as input. In these files, all information about input (a path to the 3D segmentation), output (a path to the folder where all intermediate and final output files should be stored), and parameter choices is defined. First, the number of different materials needs to be specified, followed by name tags for each material. In the following, we present our empirically chosen parameter values. For the tightening process, the radius is specified as 0.2. The number of refinement levels for medial axis points generation is 4, while the maximal sizing field is defined to be 5. We use 300 iterations of the particle system, and use at most 8 processes for parallelization, since our systems feature quad-core CPUs with hyper-threading.

Some of the pipeline steps are optimized for multi-core systems, but especially the particle system runs on a single core, resulting in very long computation times. For our meshes, as detailed in Chapter 5.3, these range from four to sixteen hours.

The resulting tetrahedral mesh can be visualized by *SCIRun*, where a one-dimensional transfer function on the material indices defines color and transparency. This is depicted in Figure 5.1.

Results

We computed many meshes from both human and pig segmentations with varying degrees of complexity. A boundary surface visualization of a pig's tho-

---

[1] http://wias-berlin.de/software/tetgen/

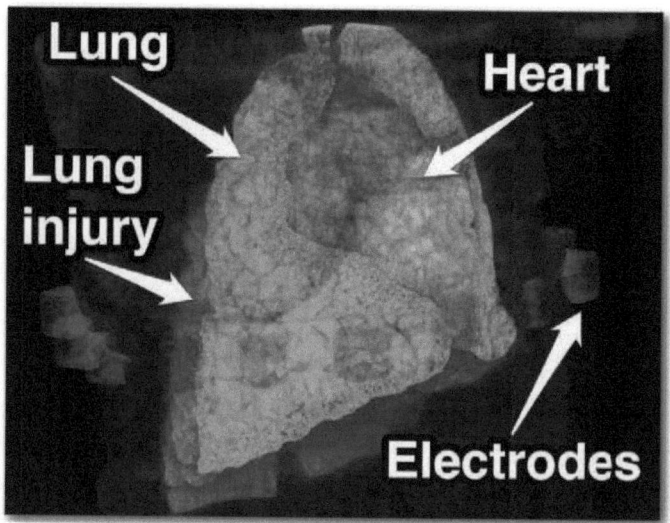

Figure 5.1: The tetrahedral mesh of a pig is visualized with *SCIRun* using a 1D transfer function on the material indices for color and transparency. Structures of interest are labeled.

rax is shown in Figure 5.2(a), which includes the lungs (yellow) and the 16 electrodes (green). Meshes with more complex structures (heart, lung damage, blood vessels) were generated for our quantitative comparison of image quality for different EIT models, which is detailed in Chapter 8. As can be seen from Figure 5.2(b), *BioMesh 3D* automatically increases the mesh density near material transitions and regions of high curvature. Vice versa, homogeneous regions feature a much coarser mesh, which results in less storage and computational effort without affecting EIT image quality. Note that it is very important for artifact reduction during image reconstruction to provide a high-density mesh near the electrodes. Since these are small structures, embedded into a different material, this adaptation is handled automatically by *BioMesh 3D*. An example of a mesh near the electrodes is shown in Figure 5.4(a).

In some rare cases, the meshing was not satisfactory due to missing components. The *BioMEsh 3D* documentation states that very small structures can be lost during the tightening step. We observed this for some very small

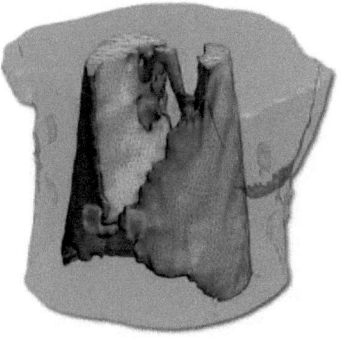 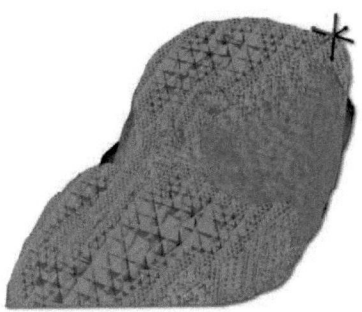

(a) Pig thorax mesh with the lung (yellow) and electrodes (green) highlighted.

(b) Interior cut of a tetrahedral mesh of the lung and heart demonstrating the adaptive mesh density.

Figure 5.2: Thorax meshes of a pig as generated by *BioMesh 3D*.

blood vessels. In addition, several larger components were ignored during the meshing, probably due to a split during tightening. We remedied this by applying a small morphological dilation to the involved materials to prevent the split of connected components.

Three-dimensional EIT models extruded from a single CT slice (called 2.5D models) are still the state-of-the-art in EIT research, and they can be generated much faster and more easily than anatomically accurate 3D models. Unfortunately, the meshing provided by *EIDORS* using *NETGEN* is very restrictive and unstable. Many electrode configurations and material combinations cause *NETGEN* to crash. Furthermore, mesh resolution is somewhat limited, as is shown in Figure 5.3(b). We therefore developed a straight-forward process to build 2.5D volume masks from a single segmentation slice as input for *BioMesh 3D*. It is very flexible in terms of materials and electrode modeling, and delivers very stable results from the meshing. Figure 5.3(a) depicts a 2.5D mesh with lung shape and accurate electrode shapes included. One drawback that we hope to improve in future work is the large mesh resolution, even in homogeneous regions. Still, we are able to produce much more precise and accurate 2.5D models compared to the current *EIDORS*-based workflow.

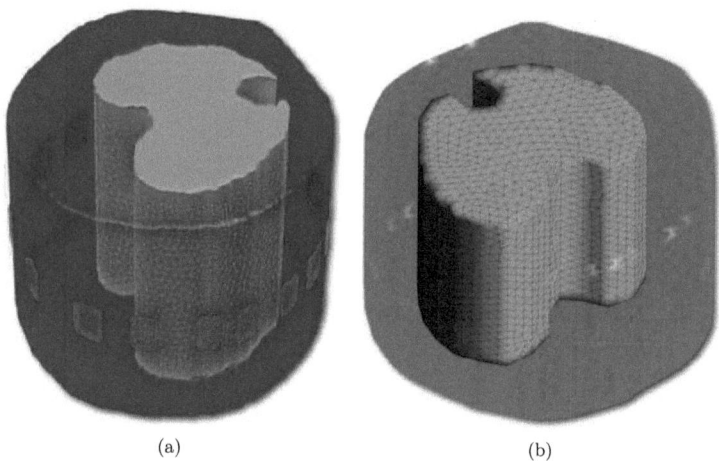

Figure 5.3: 2.5D meshes from *BioMesh 3D* (a) and *NETGEN* (b).

5.2 Final EIT Model using EIDORS

Import of BioMesh Output

The final mesh as generated by *BioMesh 3D* is stored in a file format not accessible by Matlab. Therefore, *SCIRun* is used to convert the mesh into a Matlab-compatible file. When loaded into Matlab, all nodes, tetrahedra, and material assignments are available. In order to construct an *EIDORS*-compatible forward model from this mesh, several steps are necessary as described below.

Forward Model Generation

An *EIDORS*-compatible forward model contains the nodes and elements of the mesh, along with a material assignment for each element. Furthermore, a boundary surface of the thorax is required as well as a separate set of nodes and contact impedances for all electrodes along with the conductivity distribution for each material. The data structure also contains algorithmic information such as the intended solving function and the Jacobi matrix generation. Finally, stimulation patterns need to be defined.

To compute the boundary surface of the thorax, all tetrahedra that contribute to the background or the electrodes are removed from the set and stored separately. The element list of the remaining tetrahedra is processed by the *boundary_faces* routine[2], where boundary triangles are detected as those faces which only contribute to a single tetrahedron. Nodes are centered to zero mean, and the material fields are initialized with the corresponding conductivity values for all elements.

After meshing, the 16 electrodes are no longer separated, but merged into a single material. Therefore, it is necessary to retrieve the original membership of each electrode node to a specific electrode. For this purpose, all nodes are identified that contribute to the electrode surface. These are exactly the nodes of those boundary faces of thorax and electrodes that intersect with each other (Figure 5.4(a)). The nodes are then centered to zero mean and projected to 2D using a singular value decomposition (SVD). A two-dimensional kernel density estimation (KDE) is performed, resulting in a density field with strong peaks at electrode locations (Figure 5.4(b)). These peaks are thresholded at the density field's mean value and a majority filter is applied to remove single, spurious pixels. From the resulting binary image, we determine the centroids of the 16 connected components, or raise an error if not exactly 16 components are found, see Figure 5.4(c). Since we now only have a pixel-based image of the clusters without attribution of the nodes to these clusters, we perform a k-means clustering on the projected nodes to attribute each node with the corresponding cluster ID. The clustering algorithm is robust and reliable, since we exactly know the number of clusters (16), and we can initialize it with the cluster centroids from the density field. Finally, we determine the cluster ID for each three-dimensional node of the original mesh from the projected nodes. Also, the clusters are brought into clockwise order using their polar angle to comply with *EIDORS* specifications.

A data structure for each electrode containing the mesh nodes and a contact impedance is added to the forward model. The whole mesh is re-oriented and the nodes are scaled to the $[-1, 1]^3$ volume according to the *EIDORS* specifications. Finally, stimulation patterns are generated and added to the model. Figure 5.2(a) shows a visualization of the final forward model.

---

[2]http://www.alecjacobson.com/weblog/?p=1766

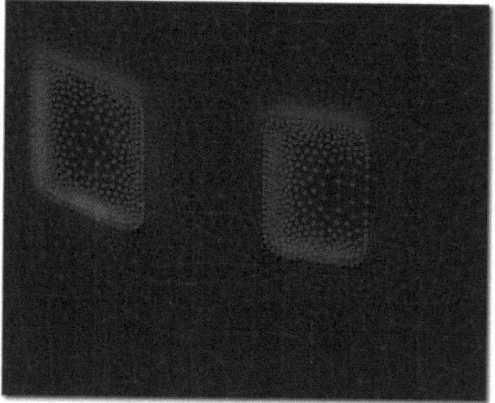

(a) Electrode nodes (red) with locally refined mesh density.

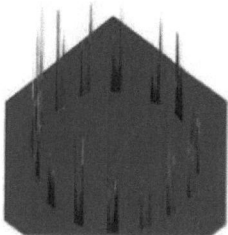 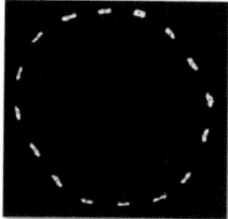

(b) Result of the kernel density estimation.

(c) Final electrode clusters (white) with centroids (red).

Figure 5.4: Electrode clustering for forward model generation.

GREIT Model

An inverse model is generated as detailed by Adler et al. [3]. Some changes to the original EIDORS code were necessary in order to process 3D meshes in contrast to the vertically homogeneous 2.5D models as explained below. Confer Chapter 3.2 for more details on the GREIT algorithm.

The first change concerns the calculation of the 2D thorax shape for the inverse model. For the 2.5D case, it is straightforward to determine the bounding box of the thorax since its shape is vertically invariant. In the 3D case, the thorax shape is more complex and might even contain protruding body parts like the front legs, which are not supposed to contribute to the bounding box near the electrode level. To determine a good bounding box for the inverse model grid, we therefore only use the thorax nodes that are at the height of the electrode belt for the grid extent. We considered the thorax shape to be sufficiently invariant for this subvolume of about 1 cm height. A resulting 2D mesh is shown in Figure 5.6(g).

The second change deals with the thorax boundary computation which is used to outline the thorax contour on the 2D reconstruction grid. The *find_boundary* routine to extract boundary triangles from the mesh delivers rough and fuzzy results (see Figure 5.5(a)). This is remedied by integrating the *boundary_faces* method, which produces the expected smooth triangle surface, as depicted in Figure 5.5(b).

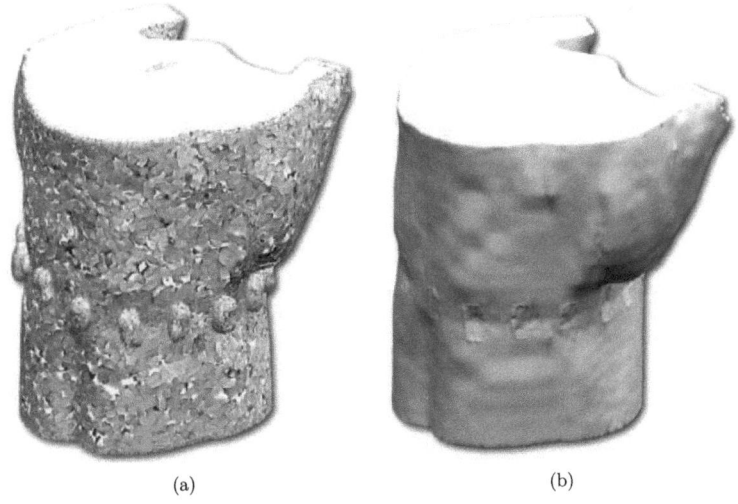

(a) (b)

Figure 5.5: Comparison of the boundary calculation according to *EIDORS* (a) and our modified implementation (b).

When scaling the input values for the conductivity targets for simulation, the original code does not incorporate the possibility of specifying minimum and maximum sizes, which should be possible according to the specification. This is fixed by using the maximum size parameter as scaling factor. Otherwise, the GREIT inverse model generation works naturally for 3D models as described in Chapter 3.2.

5.3 Summary

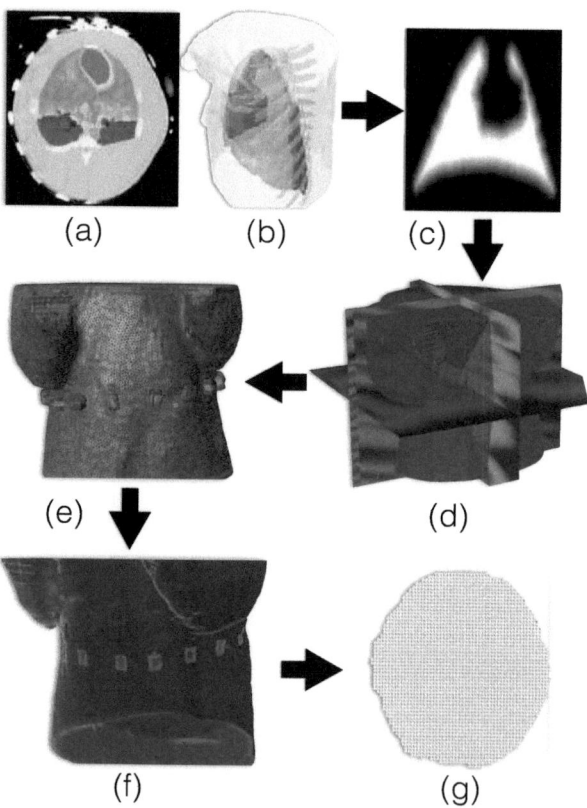

Figure 5.6: Summary of our meshing workflow. (a-b) Segmentation, (c) Tightening, (d) Distance field, (e) Particles, (f) Final mesh, (g) 2D inverse mesh.

The dominant steps of our meshing workflow are summarized in Figure 5.6. The multi-material segmentation volume mask serves as input for *BioMesh 3D* (Figure 5.6(a)-(b). The electrodes are modeled from their known shape

Dim.	Complexity	Run time Meshing	Run time GREIT	# Nodes	# Elements
2D	Circle	0.5 s	-	313	576
2D	Thorax	21 s	-	3962	7552
2D	Thorax, Lungs	27 s	-	5646	10914
2.5D	Thorax	384 s	100 s	16739	85749
2.5D	Thorax, Lungs	433 s	78 s	12650	62999
3D	Thorax	4,47 h	286 s	114910	435401
3D	Thorax, Lungs, Heart, Injury, Blood vessels	14,48 h	0,62 h	554175	2997711

Table 5.1: Runtime and mesh size comparison of 2D, 2.5D, and our 3D thorax models.

and position, which is necessary due to metal-induced noise. After separating the different materials, a tightening step is performed by *BioMesh 3D*, thereby also smoothing the rather blocky contours which result from the anisotropic volume data. This is shown in Figure 5.6(c) for a front view of the lung. Among other steps, *BioMesh 3D* computes median axes and a sizing field (Figure 5.6(d)), and initializes a particle system on material junctions and boundaries. After convergence of the particle system to a state of minimized energy (Figure 5.6(e)), the particles are used for the final mesh generation. The multi-material, multi-resolution tetrahedral mesh is converted to an *EIDORS*-compatible data structure (Figure 5.6(f)), and a forward model is calculated incorporating electrical properties of the different materials. As detailed in the next chapter, this forward model is used by the *GREIT* algorithm for training simulations. Finally, a two-dimensional grid with a precise thorax contour is calculated from the full 3D mesh for image reconstruction (Figure 5.6(g)).

Regarding computation times and mesh size, our workflow shows great potential for optimization, as outlined in the next section. A detailed comparison for the large variety of models we generated for our study is given in Chapter 8. Table 5.1 summarizes these numbers for several of our early results, including a 2D circular model, 2D as well as 2.5D models incorporating thorax and lung contours, and full 3D models, one with thorax shape only, the other with thorax, lung, and heart shape as well as pathological tissue and major blood vessels included. 2D meshes were computed with *distmesh*, 2.5D meshes with *NETGEN*, and 3D models with *BioMesh 3D*.

In conclusion, our workflow allows for the generation of complex three-dimensional EIT models in an easy, automatic, and stable way, which was not possible before. In addition, we can compute 2.5D models which are significantly superior to the state-of-the-art models as generated by *EIDORS* in terms of flexibility and complexity.

5.4 Outlook

The major drawbacks of our current workflow are twofold: First, several tools and converting steps are necessary, which is not acceptable for application in clinical research. Second, both *BioMesh 3D* and *EIDORS* are not optimized in terms of computation time and RAM usage. Especially *BioMesh 3D* is currently completely CPU-based, and the particle energy minimization is the major bottleneck of the system. Additionally, *EIDORS* works almost naturally with 3D forward models, but is not optimized for very dense and complex meshes.

A port of the particle computations for *BioMesh 3D* to the GPU was already developed [92], and first experiments indicated that computation times become up to 20 times faster. In the future, we intend to collaborate on integrating this approach into our workflow, thereby reducing mesh generation times significantly.

We also plan to optimize the *EIDORS* code for *GREIT* training, which involves many mesh perturbations. This method shows great potential for acceleration due to better memory management, parallelization, and possible GPU computations.

As described in Chapter 7.3, we are developing a multi-purpose framework based on MITK for CT segmentation, qCT calculations, and database handling. Future plans include the integration of the model generation, i.e. the interactive selection of materials, model complexity, meshing parameters, and others.

Although *BioMesh 3D* delivers high-quality meshes with specific mesh refinements and larger tetrahedra in homogeneous regions, the tetrahedra count is still very large. In the future, we will investigate methods to reduce the number of tetrahedra with a user-defined constraint on the mesh quality.

Finally, our pig CT data always includes the EIT electrode belt due to the nature of the experiments. This is a very fortunate setting, but in clinical practice, patients are not expected to wear the belt during CT scanning. We will therefore study possibilities to model the electrodes in case they are not present in the segmentation.

Chapter 6

EIT Image Reconstruction and Interpretation

Most of the available reconstruction algorithms that solve the inverse problem of calculating conductivity changes inside the thorax from voltage measurements on the skin use two-dimensional body models and are not suited for 3D models. However, the consensus algorithm *GREIT*, proposed by Adler et al. [3], is not only explicitly designed to handle 3D models, but also incorporates a sophisticated training phase using the 3D forward model to optimize certain figures of merit (compare Chapter 3.2).

We use this state-of-the-art algorithm for image reconstruction, but we also slightly adapted the code to handle 3D models, since it is optimized for the (vertically homogeneous) 2.5D models, as presented in Chapter 6.1. The resulting EIT images are compared to those reconstructed with *GREIT* and 2.5D models as well as with the common Gauss-Newton algorithm (Chapter 6.2). We present several novel insights from visually inspecting our images, while focusing on physiological effects in the thorax, certain artifacts, and the anatomical precision of the reconstruction in Chapter 6.3. In Chapter 6.4, we summarize several published image analysis and interpretation methods, together with first attempts to perform quantitative EIT calculations, and discuss the effect of using our patient-specific 3D models to gain improved results from these techniques with more confidence in their anatomical precision. Chapter 6.5 outlines our ideas and first attempts on automatically detecting time- and ventilation-invariant landmarks in both EIT and CT data to perform a registration between those very different data sets. With registration, it becomes feasible to quantify possible distortions and other artifacts from the reconstruction process and to assess the correspondence of EIT pixel clusters to anatomical structures. Finally, an outlook on future work is given in Chapter 6.6.

Parts of the results from this chapter are published as a conference abstract [139] and a paper [138].

6.1 Reconstruction using EIDORS and GREIT

In Chapter 5, we presented the generation of *EIDORS*-compatible forward and inverse models from a 3D tetrahedral mesh. The *GREIT* reconstruction algorithm [3] requires a training phase in order to minimize image distortions and artifacts. This is achieved by placing small conductivity targets of known shape and characteristics into the forward model by using mesh deformation. Solving the forward problem, i.e. calculating surface voltages from the conductivity distribution, and then reconstructing intermediate images based on these measurements, allows to quantify the image error. This process is iterated until the figures of merit are optimized.

Several parameters are required for this training phase. First, the number of training targets is defined, along with their sizes (either uniform or randomly sampled from a specified range). The position sampling can also be uniform or random. A target offset specifies whether the targets are placed in the measurement plane defined by the electrode belt or are vertically distributed. Finally, a noise figure defines the goal for convergence.

As *GREIT* is optimized for the usage of 2.5D models [10], some changes to the *EIDORS* code are necessary. We presented several modifications for forward and inverse model generation in Chapter 5.2. Additional changes to the training code include the possibility to vertically offset targets from the electrode plane. Although present in the specification, this is not very useful for 2.5D models and hence was not properly implemented in *EIDORS*. Furthermore, smaller changes were necessary to allow targets of different sizes and complex conductivity distributions for different organs.

Our first EIT images calculated from a full 3D model including lung shape

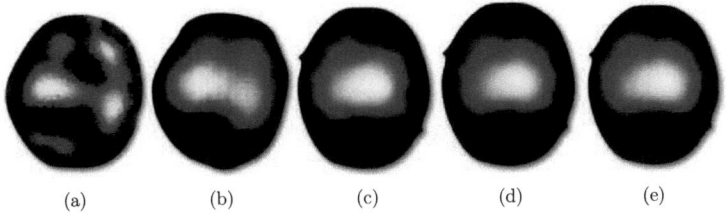

Figure 6.1: Early EIT image reconstruction results. (a) Gauss-Newton, (b) 2.5D, (c) 3D with 500 targets, (d) 3D with 5000 targets, (e) 3D with 3D target distribution.

are presented in Figure 6.1(c)-(e). We experimented with several parameter settings until the results were satisfactory. The conductivity distribution only considers thorax and lung tissue. In accordance with tutorial code from *EIDORS*[1], the lung conductivity is set to 30% of the background thorax conductivity. Confer Chapter 8 for more complex distributions incorporating more anatomical structures in the thorax. For Figure 6.1(c), the *GREIT* parameters are set to the default: image size of 64 × 64 pixels, 500 small conductivity targets with a size of 0.5% of the thorax diameter, no offset from the electrode plane, and a noise figure of 0.5. Apparently, this setting is far from optimal. The lung shape is fuzzy, and even the thorax shape is very jagged and distorted, although this is not visible here. Increasing the number of targets to 5000 resulted in Figure 6.1(d) which shows slight improvements. For Figure 6.1(e), we add a target offset of 25% of the horizontal thorax diameter. This parameter defines the maximal distance of a target from the reconstruction plane.

Comparing these images to results from a simple Gauss-Newton solver (Figure 6.1(a)), we achieve significantly less noise and a better localization of the lung activity. However, the results are far inferior to *GREIT* results from a 2.5D model, as shown in Figure 6.1(b). We investigated this unexpected outcome and discovered that the *GREIT* implementation seems to ignore the decreased contribution of lung regions with large vertical distance to the reconstruction plane. This is a possible explanation for the large conductivity

---

[1] http://eidors3d.sourceforge.net

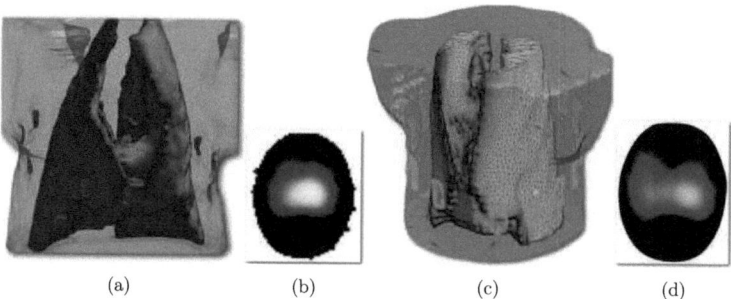

Figure 6.2: Full 3D model (a) with EIT image (b) compared to vertically clipped model (c) and EIT image (d).

changes in the thorax center. As before, this might be caused by the focus of *EIDORS* on 2.5D models where vertical homogeneity is assumed. While we will attempt to fix this issue in the future, we circumvented it by constraining the vertical extent of our 3D models to a maximum of 30% of the thorax diameter. Results are shown in Figure 6.2(c). For comparison, the whole lung model is depicted in Figure 6.2(a). Additionally, we specified training target size to randomly vary between 0.5% and 6% of the thorax diameter. With this setting, we are able to reconstruct high-quality EIT images of the lung as shown in Figure 6.2(d). These images present a better lung shape while noise is significantly reduced compared to images from the full 3D model (Figure 6.2(b)). Note that the EIT data recorded from this particular pig have a low quality in contrast to consecutive recordings, such as depicted in Figure 6.5 and presented in Chapter 8.

A summary of the data used for the results of the remainder of this chapter is presented in Figure 6.3. The 3D thorax models for two different pigs are shown to the left. The center column depicts a projection of this model into the reconstruction plane (considering the decreased contribution of remote lung regions to the EIT image). The blue contour indicates a lung shape with minimal overlap with the thorax and the heart. Finally, sample EIT images are shown to the right. We were able to record EIT measurements of high quality from the second pig (Figure 6.3(b)) which produce very accurate images with excellent lung shape.

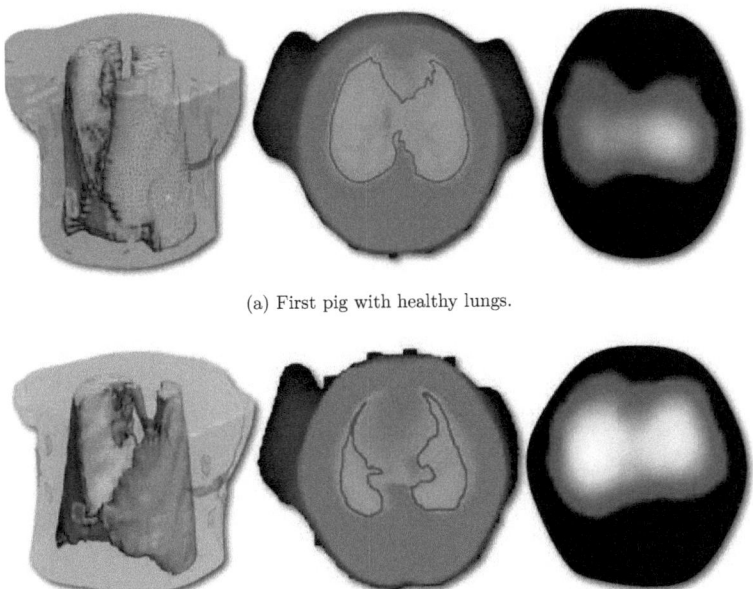

(a) First pig with healthy lungs.

(b) Second pig with prior lung injury.

Figure 6.3: Summary of our first results from 3D models. From left to right: 3D mesh, projection of lung shape into electrode plane, exemplary EIT image. Taken from [138].

6.2 Comparison to the State of Research

As published in [138], we present a visual comparison of EIT images from our 3D model including thorax and lung shape with state-of-the-art 2.5D models. To assess the anatomical precision of the lung shape, we overlay the projected 3D segmentation (center column of Figure 6.3) with the EIT images and perform a registration of the thorax shapes. Results from the first and second pig are shown in Figures 6.4 and 6.5, respectively. Each row contains an EIT data set, with the first being a baseline recording before the lung damage was induced to the pig, and the second recorded several hours after the initial injury. Additionally, we present a saline bolus injection for the second pig during a phase of apnea in the third row. Confer Chapter 6.5 and Figure 6.10(a) for

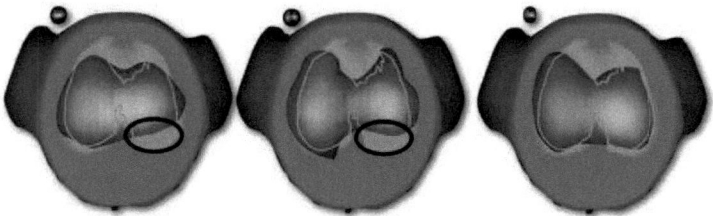

(a) Healthy lungs. Black circles mark spurious asymmetries in images from 2.5D models.

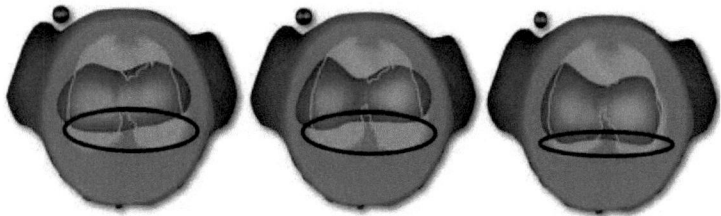

(b) After lung damage. Black circles mark non-ventilated regions.

Figure 6.4: EIT images for the first pig. Left and center: 2.5D model without and with lung shape. Right: Our 3D model. Taken from [138].

more details. The left column represents images from a 2.5D model with thorax shape only, while the center column contains a 2.5D model with included lung shape. To the right, results from our 3D models are depicted.

While a detailed report of notable insights from the results is given in Chapter 6.3, we want to point out the superior visual quality and more accurate correspondence to the anatomical lung shape.

Finally, we developed a thorax model which includes the heart shape and atelectatic lung tissue from the injury. Assigning corresponding conductivities to these structures, we use this model to reconstruct the EIT data from Figure 6.5(b). The image from a lung-only 3D model is given in Figure 6.6(a), while the result from the complex model is shown Figure 6.6(b). The anatomical heart shape is colored in red and the atelectasis is outlined in black. In comparison, it is apparent that the complex model reconstructs much smaller (if any) conductivity changes in the damaged regions, which is the expected behavior from a medical point of view. Note that this is an early result and

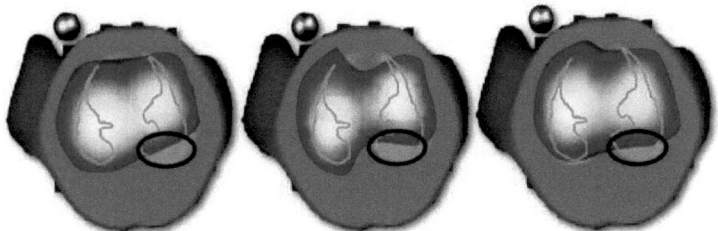

(a) Before lung damage. Black circles mark the prior lung injury.

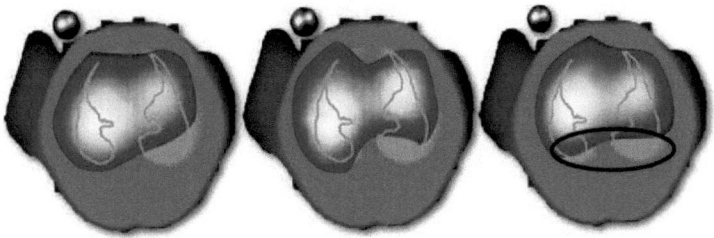

(b) After lung damage. Only our model (black circle) shows the non-ventilated regions properly.

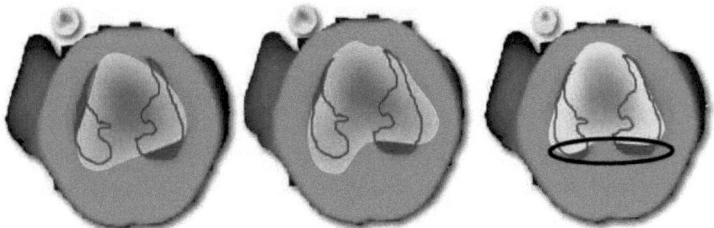

(c) Lung perfusion. The black circle in the image from our 3D model hints at a decreased perfusion in atelectatic lung regions.

Figure 6.5: EIT images for the first pig. Left and center: 2.5D model without and with lung shape. Right: Our 3D model. Taken from [138].

further studies are necessary to verify this finding.

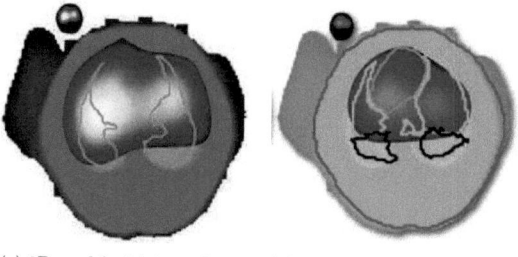

(a) 3D model with lung shape. (b) 3D model with heart shape and pathologies (black).

Figure 6.6: EIT images from 3D models with lung shape (a) and complex geometry (b).

6.3 Novel Insights due to the 3D Models

Asymmetry in Healthy Lungs

As we reported in [138], we gained several interesting insights from visually inspecting the EIT images we generated with our 3D models, and comparing them to the state-of-the-art 2.5D models. As Figure 6.4 shows, our 3D model with thorax and lung shape allows to precisely visualize the healthy lung, especially in the dorsal region (right column). In contrast, the 2.5D models both with and without lung shape delivered asymmetric images (left and center column). From the two-dimensional CT slices, and from our early works on 3D visualization of CT and EIT (compare Chapter 9), we noticed that the electrode belt of the respective pig was not planar, i.e. the electrode plane was not parallel to the axial plane due to anatomical constraints (see left column of Figure 6.3). We hypothesize that when measuring the voltages in this tilted plane, but assuming for the reconstruction that the electrodes were all in the axial plane, one side of the lung is represented with a larger volume in the image. In contrast to this, the other side contributes to a smaller volume than expected, leading to the asymmetry. With our 3D models, however, we model the electrodes at their true positions, while the reconstruction plane is identical to the 2.5D case. By incorporating this setting into the forward model and GREIT training, we assum that this would remedy the electrode plane tilt, resulting in the expected parallel dorsal lung boundary. Since discussions about this effect, its cause, and its consequences were lengthy and difficult due to the different background and habits of computer scientists and medical researchers, we developed a 3D visualization with the goal of improving visual communication. This effort is detailed in Chapter 9. Only recently, during our work on the study presented in Chapter 8, we discovered that the asymmetry in the 2.5D images was in fact caused by wrongly ordered electrodes in the *EIDORS* code, resulting in a rotation of the image by

$$\frac{1}{16} \cdot 360° = 22.5°. \qquad (6.1)$$

Prior Lung Injury

In contrast to the asymmetry reported above, which was only visible in the 2.5D images and turned out to be an artifact, a different data set exhibits an asymmetry in images from both 2.5D and 3D models, as can be seen in Figure 6.5(a)-(b). This EIT data was recorded in the baseline phase before any artificial lung injury, so we expected the images to look similar to the ones reported above. After many discussions and inspections of the data (both the CT slices and preliminary 3D visualizations of the CT data augmented with the segmentation), we attributed the asymmetry to a prior lung injury of the pig, which was not noticed before. This poorly ventilated lung tissue was present in both sides of the lung, but more dominant on the right side, and especially in the lower dorsal lung regions. As Figure 6.3(b) shows, the electrode belt is placed rather low due to anatomical constraints, almost below the heart. This causes lower lung regions to contribute more than usual to the EIT image. It is therefore a reasonable conclusion that the asymmetry in the EIT image is caused by this prior lung injury. This finding increases our confidence in the anatomical precision of our 3D models, since the effect can be observed much better with our model than with the 2.5D models. Also, the lung boundary in a healthy pig is very accurate, so one can assume that all asymmetries detected in the dorsal lung regions of EIT images are caused by events inside the lung, and not by artifacts or inaccuracies.

Lung Perfusion in the Presence of Atelectasis

Our third finding is concerned with a data set recorded after the lung injury was induced, during a phase of apnea, where a saline bolus was injected into the heart to increase blood conductivity. With this method, it is possible to visualize lung perfusion, which produces conductivity changes that are about two magnitudes lower than the ventilation signal. An overlay with the lung shape indicates that the dorsal atelectatic regions are significantly less perfused than aerated lung regions, see Figure 6.3(c). From the medical point of view, this is not surprising, since atelectatic lung regions do not participate in oxygen exchange. Hence, blood flow to these regions is reduced or redirected to aerated lung regions. The anatomical precision of the 3D model and the findings described above made us confident enough to draw such a conclusion from the image data. This shows that 3D models can support perfusion analysis of EIT images significantly, which is a very promising research area (see also the next sections).

6.4 Impact on EIT Analysis Methods

As already sketched in Chapters 3.2 and 3.3, there are many efforts to derive clinically useful quantitative information from EIT images. While a certain degree of success was reported, the significance of EIT data depends strongly on the thorax model used for image reconstruction. This is especially apparent for the *RVD* index [111], depicted in Figure 3.1 of Chapter 3.3. It is only useful to apply this method if a good estimate of the dorsal lung boundary is known. Otherwise, it is impossible to discriminate atelectatic lung regions from surrounding soft tissue without performing a *PEEP* titration since both display hardly any conductivity changes during ventilation.

We classify EIT interpretation approaches into four categories and outline the impact of our improved thorax models for these methods.

One group of publications deals with an important clinical task for treatment of ARDS patients (compare Chapter 3.1). As mechanically ventilated patients are vulnerable to ventilator-induced injury such as lung collapse and overdistension, EIT can support the monitoring and adjustment of ventilation parameters, for example the *PEEP*. Costa et al. [36] estimate recruitable lung collapse and overdistended regions by a pixel-wise compliance comparison during PEEP titration. Wolf et al. [167] study the overdistension at large tidal volumes, which are required for collapse reduction in horizontal regions of interest. Gómez-Laberge et al. [67] estimate the Dynamic Respiratory System Compliance as well as overdistension and atelectasis pixel by pixel. Becher et al. [14] also estimate tidal recruitment overdistension during *PEEP* titration. Muders et al. [111] apply the Regional Ventilation Delay Index (RVD) to assess tidal recruitment during a lowflow inflation maneuver. Reifferscheid et al. [127] study the influence of posture and measurement plane on EIT images. Elke et al. [51] attempt to validate EIT for regional ventilation distribution estimation by comparison to xenon CT data.

A second group of publications study the treatment of pneumothoraces using EIT. Costa et al. [37] automatically detect and locate a pneumothorax and distinguish it from overdistension of similar appearance. Preis et al. [118] report the monitoring of a tension pneumothorax and its behavior by EIT imaging.

EIT image segmentation is pursued by several research groups. Grychtol et al. [75] develop an event detection method based on fuzzy logic to automatically detect openings, collapse, overdistension and recovering of lung regions. Gómez-Laberge et al. [68] apply a fuzzy k-means classification of ventilated lung tissue. Ferrario et al. [57] present an automatic detection of heart and lung regions in EIT images and quantify the overlap with anatomically accurate CT data.

Finally, Czaplik et al. [41] compare several EIT parameters in terms of usefulness for *PEEP* optimization.

The last group of publications study the lung perfusion as a secondary signal component in EIT data. Frerichs et al. [61] assess lung perfusion changes on a coarse scale for the left and right lung regions. Fagerberg et al. [54] estimate the V/Q ratio, i.e. the matching of ventilation and pulmonary perfusion. Maisch et al. [103] study the ability of EIT to estimate stroke volume variation for heart-lung interactions. Borges et al. [18] use a saline bolus injection for regional lung perfusion estimation. Finally, Proença et al. [119] study the effect of heart motion on perfusion data from EIT.

In summary, all of these works advance the applicability of EIT to the treatment of ventilated patients. However, most authors admit that a rather detailed knowledge of the pixels contributing to the lung is required. As this knowledge is currently not available, approximations are used such as *PEEP* titration or thresholding of pixel values. Our 3D thorax models improve the quality and expressiveness of EIT images and allow for higher confidence in the analysis methods presented in this section, since they pave the way for determining the lung boundary.

6.5 Landmark Detection and Registration with CT

Anatomical Landmarks in EIT

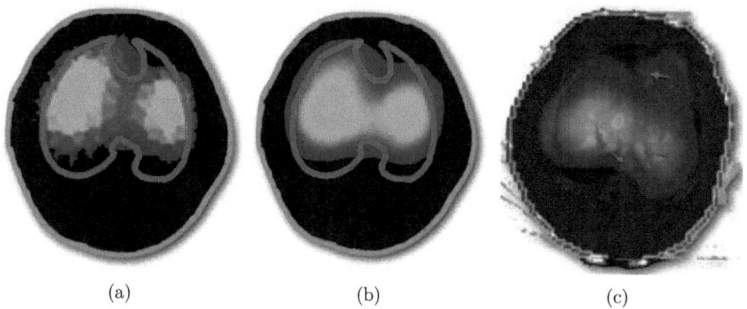

(a)   (b)   (c)

Figure 6.7: Displacement of EIT pixels in 2D (a) vs. 3D (b) models and anatomical landmarks (c).

In order to assess the anatomical accuracy of EIT image structures and to study the degree of distortions, we propose a landmark-based registration with CT data. Many causes influence the image quality and precision of EIT such as simplified or imprecise thorax models and the linearized solvers for the ill-posed non-linear problem of image reconstruction. As depicted in Figure 6.7, the lung shapes in EIT images from a simple 2D thorax model (a) and a complex 3D model with multiple anatomical structures (b) appear quite similar. These images are results from our study presented in Chapter 8.

Note that the difference in terms of smoothness is caused by a difference in reconstruction mesh resolution. Conversely, the regions of large conductivity change (green) are at different locations, which demonstrates the effect of distortion from simplified models.

As mentioned before, determining the dorsal lung boundary in the presence of atelectasis is a critically important application of EIT. A registration with CT data is expected to increase confidence in methods that attempt to solve this task.

There are several notable differences between CT and EIT (compare Chapter 2). A functional difference-EIT image shows a lens-shaped projection of conductivity changes into the measurement planes. CT on the other hand is an anatomically accurate 3D imaging technique with a 64 times larger number of pixels in a single slice. It does not incorporate functional and dynamical information.

In order to achieve a registration between these very different data sets, we propose several time- and ventilation-invariant landmarks which can be detected in both CT and EIT images. In addition, instead of using a single CT slice as a reference (for example [57]), we attempt to mimic the projection from 3D to the EIT measurement plane for the CT slices. Thus, we hope to get a 2D representation of the CT data which matches the expected EIT lung shape more closely (confer the center column of Figure 6.3).

The obvious candidates for ventilation-invariant landmarks are large blood vessels and the heart, since they hardly change their location over time. Although regional lung perfusion can be affected by ventilation, the pulmonary arteries do not move significantly. The heart is the second largest source of thoracic conductivity changes and also a structure large enough to be easily located in EIT. The descending aorta is the largest blood vessel in the thorax and runs almost vertical in humans. Hence, a circular-shaped projection into an EIT image is expected. Also, the aorta is a good spatial indicator of the dorsal lung boundary. Finally, the main bronchia are sufficiently location-invariant and are assumed to be easily recognizable in EIT. Figure 6.7 depicts an overlap of EIT and CT data based on thorax shape registration (see below) with these landmarks highlighted by arrows.

Perfusion-related Signal Separation

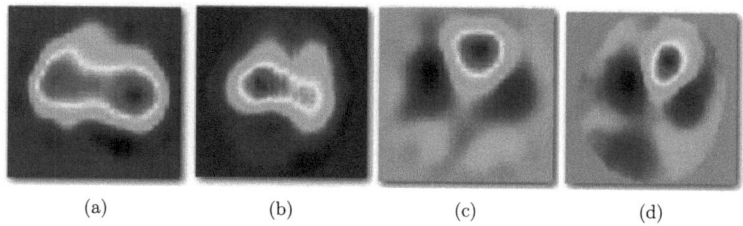

(a)　　　　　　(b)　　　　　　(c)　　　　　　(d)

Figure 6.8: First and second principal components of EIT signals from Dräger (a,c) and 2.5D (b,d) models.

Several attempts have been made to separate the ventilation from the cardiac signals [44, 117, 57, 125]. We used the method by Deibele et al. [44] because it allows to extract the pulmonary perfusion signal in addition to cardiac activity, although this is about two magnitudes smaller than the ventilation signal and overlaps with it. This decomposition is achieved by performing a Principal Component Analysis (PCA) and fitting template functions derived from the principal components (PC) to the data. Figure 6.8 depicts the first and second principal components from EIT data reconstructed with the Dräger model [152] (a,c) and with a 2.5D model (b,d). Clearly, the first PC contains mostly ventilation signals, while the heart contributes significantly to the second PC. A successful signal separation is presented in Figure 6.9(a), demonstrating also the difference in signal amplitude. Figure 6.9(b) depicts the perfusion signal at the assumed aorta location, showing good resemblance to the actual cardiac signal as known from ECG measurements.

As this kind of signal separation is still in early research, the state-of-the-art procedure in clinical research for perfusion analysis is the injection of a saline bolus of high conductivity into the heart during a phase of apnea. Such a maneuver is shown in Figure 6.10(a). Several breaths before (1) and after (5) the maneuver, a phase of apnea (2), saline bolus injection (3) and diffusion of the bolus (4) are depicted. This allows for an EIT recording of thorax perfusion without the distracting ventilation signal. An example image is given in Figure 6.10(c). In comparison, we show results from the signal separation during

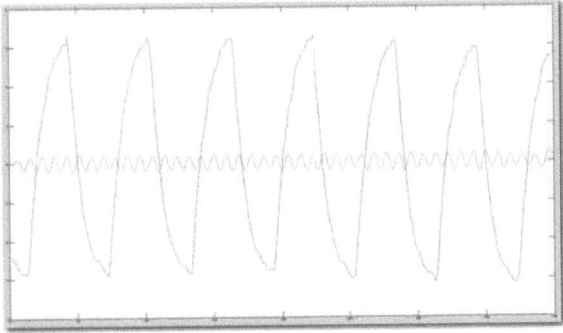

(a) Signal separation of ventilation (blue) and perfusion (green).

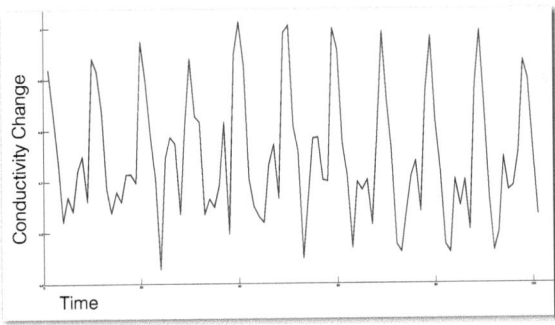

(b) Perfusion signal correlating with cardiac activity.

Figure 6.9: EIT signal separation and perfusion information.

ventilation for lung perfusion in Figure 6.10(b). In Chapter 8 we demonstrate that the saline bolus is not superior to the signal separation in terms of heart segmentation. Finally, Figure 6.11 shows the different phases of thorax perfusion during saline bolus injection, i.e. the blood flow from the heart to the pulmonary arteries and the aorta (a), the rough location of the pulmonary arteries (b), and the heart (c).

Localization of the Descending Aorta

Detection of the descending aorta is a challenging task due to its small size versus the spatial resolution of EIT and its weak signal compared to venti-

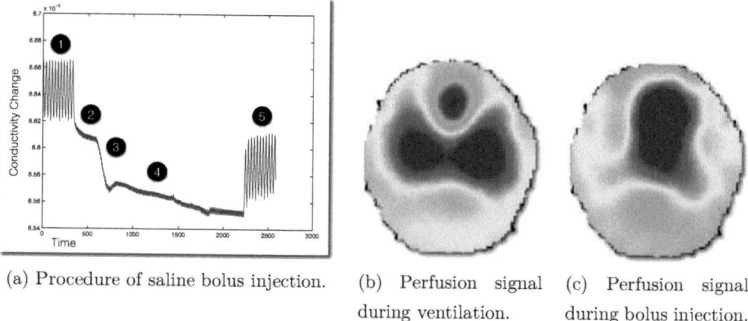

(a) Procedure of saline bolus injection. (b) Perfusion signal during ventilation. (c) Perfusion signal during bolus injection.

Figure 6.10: Saline bolus injection to enhance blood conductivity.

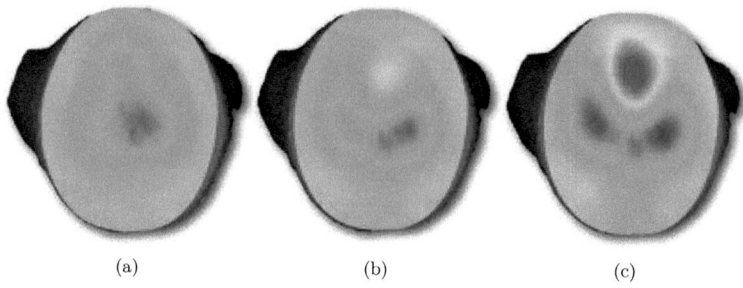

(a) (b) (c)

Figure 6.11: Different phases of the saline bolus injection. (a) Blood flow from heart to aorta and pulmonary arteries. (b) Lung perfusion. (c) Heart beat.

lation and cardiac activity. Two works by Solà et al. [146, 145] attempt to locate the aorta in EIT data to estimate pulse arrival time and central blood pressure. They inject the saline bolus directly into the aorta to circumvent the heart and pulmonary arteries. Additionally, they measure ECG data to isolate perfusion-specific signals in the EIT image. Braun et al. [23] compare different electrode belt positions to determine an optimal measurement plane for aorta localization.

While we will study the performance of the aorta detection by Solà et al. [145] in the future, we are able to distinguish different phases of perfusion from the time shift compared to the heart signal (blue plot in Figure 6.12(a)). The slightly shifted lung perfusion is given in green and the aorta signal in

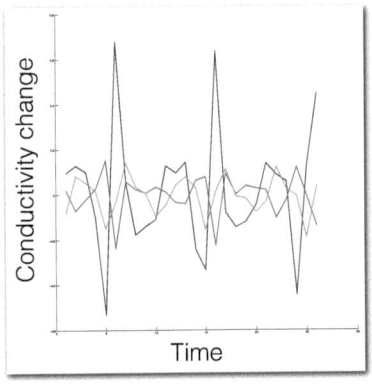 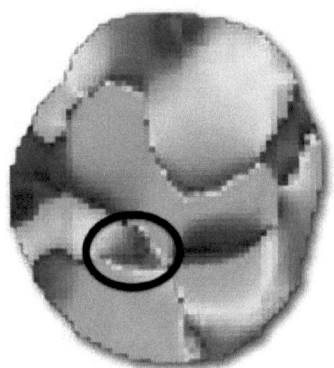

(a) Phase difference of lung (red) and aorta (green) regions comopared to the heart (blue).

(b) Phase image with the assumed aorta location highlighted.

Figure 6.12: Proposed aorta detection method based on signal phase.

red. These are averaged signals gathered from manually determined regions of interest. We calculated the phase shift for each EIT image pixel compared to the heart and visualized it as shown in Figure 6.12(b). While these are preliminary results, the image indicates a small region of significantly different phase (red, highlighted with a black circle) compared to surrounding regions and lung (blue). The location of this region coincides well with the expected aorta position, although further research is necessary to validate this finding.

Another preliminary result from our studies of thorax perfusion in EIT is given in Figure 6.13. Similar to the approach by Deibele et al. [44], we extracted several principal components (PC) from a saline bolus data set. While the following is just a hypothesis, the spatial agreement of EIT structures with the actual blood vessels is intriguing. We suspect that the first PC shown on the top left represents the heart, while the second PC can be attributed to lung perfusion (bottom left). The third PC coincides strongly with the venous reflux from the vena cava (top right). Finally, the bottom right image could show the blood flow through the aortic arch. We are excited by this finding and hope to verify our hypothesis in future work.

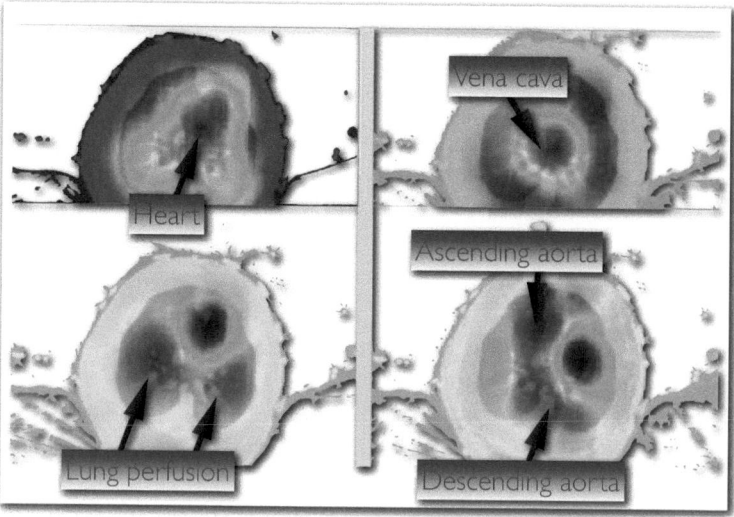

Figure 6.13: Our hypothesis regarding the different principal components of the perfusion signal. Strong conductivity changes (red) seem to correlate well with the anatomical location of blood vessels.

EIT/CT Registration

As described in Chapter 8, our registration between EIT and CT is currently limited to the thorax shape to achieve at least a rough overlap. Several works on registration of different medical image modalities are worth investigating, such as lung registration [50], fusion of ultrasound and CT [164, 52], and registration of endoscopic images to CT data [174]. In addition, basic landmark-based image registration methods will be investigated for future work.

6.6 Outlook

In our next steps regarding EIT image reconstruction, we will pursue several optimization approaches. First, we plan to accelerate the *GREIT* training code in *EIDORS* to work with large tetrahedral meshes and many simulation targets. The current non-optimized code requires more than 30 GB of memory and takes up to 40 minutes. Second, we will investigate recent findings by

Zhao et al. [178] regarding the dependence of lung tissue captured by EIT on the position of the measurement plane. Also, Zhao et al. [176] state that the *GREIT* algorithm is sensitive to conductivity targets near the thorax boundary, and Gaggero et al. [63] propose a method to improve *GREIT* by using real data instead of simulations for training.

While we entertained the idea to use independent component analysis instead of PCA for signal separation for several years, Rahman et al. [125] were the first to publish such a method. We hope to achieve an improved and more stable separation of perfusion and ventilation components from EIT images with this approach.

Finally, we are intrigued by early attempts on EIT image segmentation [75, 68]. Hence, we will focus our future image interpretation work on this research area.

Chapter 7

Additional Collaborations with Medical Researchers

In this chapter, three smaller projects in the scope of Electrical Impedance Tomography and quantitative Computed Tomography are presented. Medical researchers need to generate, process, store, and analyze very large amounts of data for their studies, especially if 3D images are involved. In our case, data from animal experiments involving pigs, clinical CT scans from the University Hospital of Leipzig as well as from other collaborators are available. Much of the data processing is currently done manually and with the help of a variety of different software tools, which is cumbersome and error-prone. Thus, thorough inspection is necessary, increasing the processing time even more.

Although no new algorithms were developed for these projects, the collaboration between computer scientists and medical researchers resulted in a much faster data processing and analysis. Furthermore, it will spawn several medical journal publications. Progress in qCT and EIT research is also accelerated, since more data can be analyzed, less manual inspection is necessary, and experimentation is possible in a faster and easier fashion. All three projects are either not yet completed or part of larger projects, so this chapter will present the setting and preliminary results. Several journal publications reporting the results from the medical point of view are underway.

A setting where computer scientists and medical researchers with a computational interest work together on clinically relevant topics is very fruitful, improved even more by the unique amount of clinical data available in our team.

In Chapter 7.1, we demonstrate how the extraction of ten slices from a thorax CT can be performed automatically for a large number of data sets, along with the computation of qCT measurements and storage of the results in Excel sheets. Chapter 7.2 describes a similar project to study the usefulness of CT subvolumes with different heights for qCT calculations. Finally, Chapter 7.3 shows our first efforts to develop a multi-purpose software platform with the focus on CT segmentation, along with the vision for future workflow integration.

7.1 Ten Slice Extrapolation

Problem Formulation and Collaboration

In clinical practice, intensive care treatment of lung patients usually requires several CT scans of the whole thorax. Before the treatment, one data set is recorded to visually determine the state of the lung and possible treatment strategies. Depending on the development of the patient's state, several control scans are performed during the next days. This requires the storage and processing of a very large amount of data and exposes the patient to a significant amount of radiation. Furthermore, cumbersome manual work is necessary to delineate the lung boundary in the presence of pathology, since automated procedures cannot handle this setting (confer Chapter 4). As quantitative CT calculations get more and more important in clinical research and are promising for patient data use, it is crucial to develop software-based methods for processing the data automatically to ensure timely availability.

As published by our medical collaborators, the amount of CT data can be reduced by using only ten evenly-spaced slices of the lung [130]. They report that this subset is representative for the whole lung in terms of quantitative CT measurements like mass, volume and gas content. In [129], Reske et al. present a validation study on sheep and pig data using Bland-Altman plots [15], reporting a bias of less than 1% of the total lung mass and volume, and a level of agreement of up to 2.5%. This indicates that not only can data processing and storage be reduced significantly, but also the radiation exposure and recording time for the patient. In Figure 7.1, these ten slices are depicted for a sample data set on the left hand side. The right hand side shows the lung approximation by constant interpolation from the ten slices.

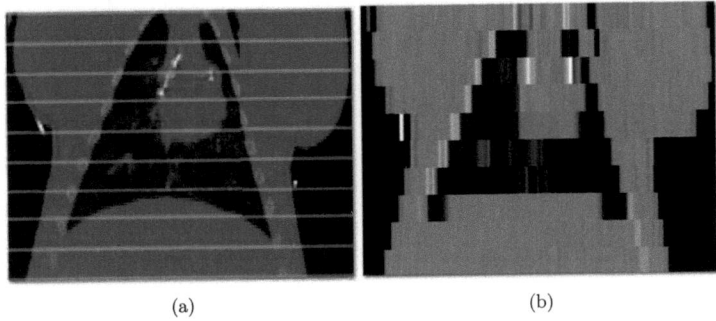

Figure 7.1: Selection of ten evenly spaced slices (a) and constant interpolation as an approximation of the lung (b).

The current workflow for qCT analysis and slice extraction comprises different software tools and manual processing steps. The *Osiris* software is used to delineate the lung boundary in each slice. The segmentation is exported to the *Luva* tool, which performs the qCT calculations and writes the results into an Excel sheet. This process needs to be repeated for each data set, after which the results are manually aggregated in a single Excel sheet for further analysis. The ten representative slices are currently extracted manually from the DICOM files and loaded into *Luva* separately.

This slice extraction is especially cumbersome and error-prone since DICOM header information such as the slice thickness needs to be considered. Also, the calculation of the slices' indices need to be performed manually. The ten segmented slices are loaded into the *Luva* tool which calculates the qCT measurements for each single slice. The results are stored in an Excel sheet, which is then used to semi-automatically compute the extrapolation. We have hundreds of previously segmented CT data sets available, comprising tens of thousands of individual images. A manual slice extraction, analysis, and inspection requires several weeks of work for a small team of medical researchers. With the help of automated software, this process can be completed in a few

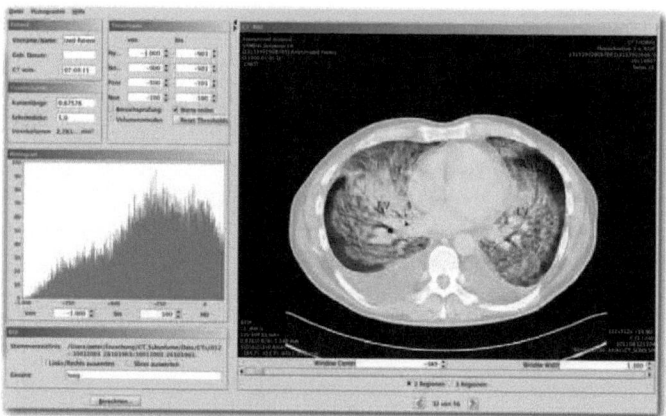

Figure 7.2: A screenshot of the *Luva* software, showing a segmented CT slice and the corresponding histogram.

hours.

Data and Requirements

Our data set comprises almost 1000 thorax CT scans from patients with a wide variety of pathologies. The images are collected from several clinical centers with different devices, settings, and parameters like filtering and slice thickness. Our software thus needs to be very general in terms of data handling to avoid program errors and miscalculations. Since the intended users are medical researchers, the software is required to be intuitive as well as robust and reliable.

In a preliminary step, a consistent nomenclature for all data sets was required. Naturally, the different clinical centers each had their own folder structure and naming scheme. We developed a nomenclature that is suitable for automated processing, easy to read for the medical user, and which requires minimal conversion from the original structures. All data sets were converted to the new standard, which only took about 50 ms per CT scan on a fast computer with a flash-based hard drive.

Name	From (HU)	To (HU)	Color
Hyperventilated	-1000	-901	Blue
Normal	-900	-501	Yellow
Poor	-500	-101	Orange
Non-ventilated	-100	+100	Purple

Table 7.1: Voxel classification based on the Hounsfield scale.

Methodology

User interaction with our software is designed to be minimal: From a GUI dialogue, the user selects the parent folder of all data sets to be processed. The DICOM images for each patient are stored in separate folders. In most cases, several CT scans are available for each patient at different times, for example before and after the treatment. These are stored in their own folders inside the patient's main folder. For experimentation, it is possible to change the number of slices to be extracted, which the user can do graphically.

Two progress bars will inform the user about the current patient and the current patient-specific data set. For each scan, the segmented CT images are loaded and the polygons enclosing the lung tissue are converted to a volume mask.

Since an automatic determination of the first and last slice of interest containing lung tissue is virtually impossible, user interaction is necessary. As shown in Figure 7.3, the user can set the windowing function of the grayscale range and scroll through the slices in an axial view. By clicking the corresponding buttons, the first and last slices are chosen. The remaining eight slices are computed using the slice thickness parameter in the DICOM header. The optimal slice positions usually do not match real slices, so the closest slice to a position is chosen. These slices are then stored in a separate folder as DICOM files for future use. The streamlined interface on the right hand side allows for a fast and intuitive processing.

Each voxel inside the lung volume mask is classified using a standard approach: Depending on their Hounsfield value (HU), voxels can represent overdistended, non-, poorly, or normally ventilated lung tissue (compare Table 7.1 and Figure 7.4). Voxels outside of the HU range are discarded.

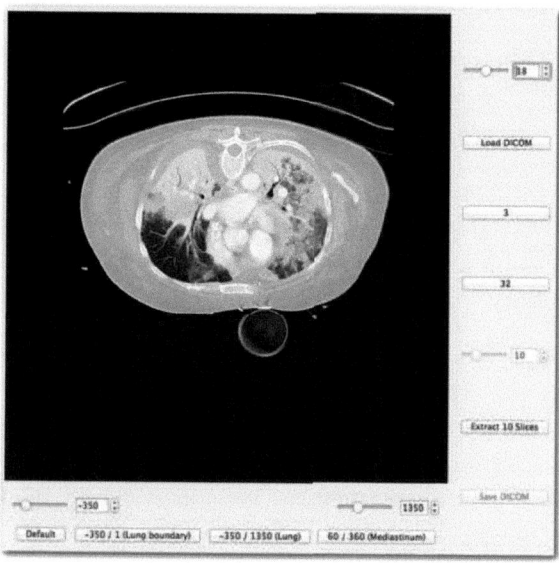

Figure 7.3: The software prototype for extraction of the ten slices. The user is guided by the order of the buttons on the right hand side.

The volume of a single voxel (measured in $[ml]$) is known from the DICOM header as

$$V_{Voxel} = ps_x \cdot ps_y \cdot st \cdot 0.001. \tag{7.1}$$

Here, ps_x and ps_y specify pixel spacing and st the slice thickness in $[cm]$. The volume of all voxels belonging to a certain tissue classification can be calculated trivially. The mass in $[g]$ for all voxels is computed as

$$M_{all} = \sum_{i=1}^{N} (1 + 0.001 \cdot HU_i) \cdot V_{Voxel}. \tag{7.2}$$

N is the number of all voxels and HU_i the Hounsfield value of the ith voxel. The voxel subsets are computed in the same way. For each subset, the relative mass and volume with respect to the whole lung is also computed. The relative

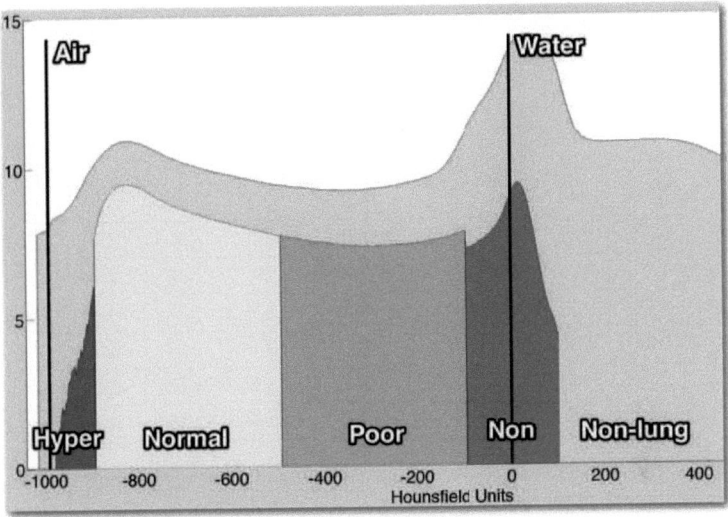

Figure 7.4: Annotated histogram of the lung with standard classification.

gas content, i.e. the fraction of air inside the lung, is given by

$$GC_r = \frac{1}{-1000} \cdot \frac{1}{N} \cdot \sum_{i=1}^{N} HU_i. \tag{7.3}$$

The Hounsfield value assigned to air is -1000. The absolute gas content is then $GC_a = GC_r \cdot V_{all}$.

The calculations are performed for each slice, which represents a certain subvolume of the lung specified by the slice thickness. All results are stored in a table with each row containing all relative and absolute measurements for a certain slice. The so-called extrapolation for the space between two slices is performed according to the equation given by Reske et al. [130], here for the volume:

$$V_{ext}(i) = d \cdot \frac{V_i + V_{i+1}}{2 \cdot st}. \tag{7.4}$$

In this equation, i is the slice number, and d is the absolute difference between the positions of slices i and $i+1$.

Finally, the approximated measurements for the whole lung are computed

No.	Slice pos.	st	M_{total}	M_{non}	M_{poor}	M_{norm}	M_{hyper}
1	-347	6	0,84	0,84	0,00	0,00	0,00
2	-323	6	11,16	11,14	0,02	0,00	0,00
3	-299	6	25,97	20,89	3,37	1,72	0,00
4	-269	6	55,18	22,61	20,59	11,97	0,00
5	-239	6	39,56	15,93	12,54	11,08	0,00
6	-209	6	21,23	9,20	8,11	3,91	0,00
7	-179	6	12,00	4,50	5,26	2,25	0,00
8	-155	6	6,16	0,46	2,65	3,04	0,00
9	-131	6	3,32	0,11	0,74	2,48	0,00
10	-107	6	0,54	0,03	0,41	0,10	0,00
Lung Extrapolated			851,93	413,74	260,65	177,54	0,00

Table 7.2: Example for the extrapolation output. Measurements in [%].

as

$$V_{extrapolated} = \frac{1}{2} \cdot V_1 + \frac{1}{2} \cdot V_{10} + \sum_{i=1}^{9} V_{ext}(i). \qquad (7.5)$$

Since the extrapolated relative values are not meaningful, they are recalculated from the new extrapolated absolute values. Note that in contrast to the naming scheme, the performed operation is actually closer to a constant interpolation.

A shortened example for the extrapolation excel sheet is shown in Table 7.2. It is constrained to absolute mass measurements only, but the full table also contains volume data as well as relative values (with respect to the total mass and volume). The slice position and thickness are given in [mm], and the mass is given in [g].

If a previous, manually created Excel sheet is available, it is loaded to be compared to the automated results. A warning is raised only if a difference greater than 1 ml or 1 g is detected, since smaller errors are not significant and might stem from a different conversion of the lung boundary polygon to a volume mask in the *Luva* tool.

The table is stored as an Excel sheet in a standardized way, along with the difference table, if applicable.

Results

As several hundred CT scans have already been manually processed, the resulting table was compared to our automated results. The objectives were to both verify our code, and to detect errors in the data. Fortunately, only very few cases were found where the manually created results differed significantly from the automated results, i.e more than a few grams or milliliters. This demonstrates the high quality work performed by our medical collaborators.

Assuming that the CT scan is already segmented, the interactive extraction of the ten slices is the main bottleneck of our workflow. The whole data set has to be inspected, and it is sometimes difficult to quickly determine the first and last slices containing lung tissue. Thus, this step takes about 40 to 60 seconds for each scan. The extrapolation from the ten slices takes only 1.6 seconds (loading the DICOM slices, stacking them to a volume, including the segmented lung mask, computing qCT measurements for each slice, performing the extrapolation, comparing the result to the manually created file, and storing the new table into an Excel sheet), where the DICOM loading requires about 75% of that time.

Impact

As reported in the previous section, our automated approach requires significantly less time for slice extraction, qCT calculations, and data aggregation, while much less effort for inspection and correction is needed. Since our database of CT scans grows rapidly, the time savings are very crucial for current and future research. Also, the code can be generalized for other calculations and data sets, as described for example in Chapter 7.2.

Future Work

As detailed in Chapter 7.3, we are developing a multi-purpose software platform with the main focus on lung segmentation in thorax CT scans. We plan to extend the features of this platform towards processing and archiving of our large amount of data, extraction of certain slices and subvolumes as well as qCT calculations. Our vision is to only use one software framework for most of the computational workflows in CT and EIT lung research. While our current implementation as described above was developed in Matlab, the code can be easily ported to and integrated into other platforms.

7.2 Study concerning CT subvolume regions of interest

Problem Formulation

This project is a collaboration with Dr. A. W. Reske and U. Oesch from the University Hospital of Leipzig. My contribution comprises the development of an automatic processing and analysis software and the support during the statistical analysis.

Similar to the extrapolation project presented in Chapter 7.1, our research question is whether a subvolume of the lung with specific height is representative for the whole lung in terms of qCT precision. Again, this would result in less data handling and storage, less segmentation effort, and less radiation exposure of the patient.

This work was inspired by our and other researchers' experience with Electrical Impedance Tomography. A lens-shaped volume of 6-10 cm height contributes most prominently to an EIT image in the electrode plane. Thus, we are interested whether such a volume is representative for the whole lung not only for EIT, but also for qCT measurements. As our results presented in Chapter 8 indicate, such subvolumes might also be a suitable 3D thorax model for EIT imaging.

Previous Work

This work was mostly inspired by previous research by Reske et al. [130, 131, 129], as described in Chapter 7.1. The authors report that ten evenly spaced CT slices are representative for the whole lung in terms of qCT measurements including volume, mass, and gas content. Also, EIT researchers agree that only a certain subvolume around the electrode plane contributes significantly to EIT images. Thus, if our study indicated that a subvolume of a similar height is representative for the whole lung, this would also deliver important implications for EIT imaging.

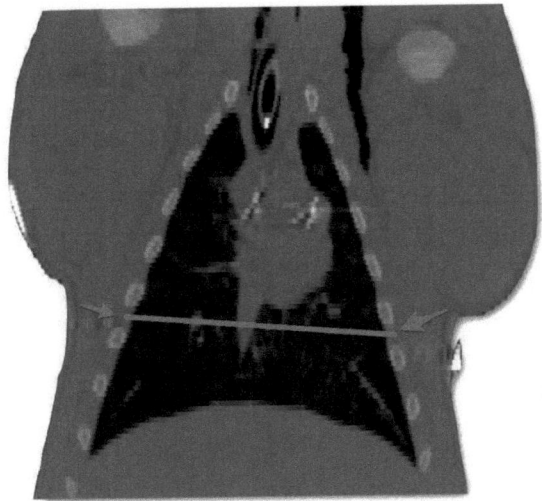

Figure 7.5: The fifth inter-costal space corresponding to the baseline for subvolume calculation.

Preliminary work on this project was done by Ulrike Oesch during her dissertation project. A literature search showed that the most frequently used location for the EIT electrode belt is the fifth inter-costal space (ICR), although sometimes anatomical constrains require a different placement. This is often the case for women or morbidly obese patients. Thus, Oesch manually determined the CT slice closest to the fifth ICR in thorax CT scans for 159 patients. Figure 7.5 shows an example. Furthermore, she extracted subvolumes of 1, 2, 3, 4, and 5 cm above and below this ICR slice manually, stored them separately, and calculated qCT measurements using the *Luva* tool. Results were aggregated in an Excel sheet for further analysis.

My task in this project began with the verification of the extracted CT slices, the qCT measurements, and the Excel sheet, while also accelerating the whole workflow for current and future use with an automated software that is usable by medical researchers.

Data

The data set for this study consists of thorax CT scans of 159 patients. The patients are organized in three groups: The first group (89 individuals) suffers from severe lung damage caused by ARDS. The second group (43 individuals) is mechanically ventilated, but had no lung injury before the treatment. The third group (27 individuals) is spontaneously breathing, also without lung injury.

The following statistics were recorded: age, sex, height, and number of CT slices for the whole lung. These are summarized in Table 7.3 for the whole data set as well as for each group. Note that minor patients were also included in this study since they contribute to a representative set of patients who undergo lung treatment. For each patient, a segmented thorax CT of the whole lung is available. Thus, it is possible to compare the qCT calculations of all subvolumes to the true properties of the lung.

Since the data was recorded using different CT devices, different filtering settings, slice numbers, and slice thickness, the overall quality of the images can diverge significantly. Also, a robust data handling is necessary.

Analysis

As in Chapter 7.1, the qCT measurements of interest are mass, volume, and gas content for each of the different lung tissue classes, i.e. normally ventilated, poorly ventilated, non-ventilated, and hyper-ventilated. In contrast to the approximation of the whole lung by just ten slices, we only consider a subvolume of the lung. Therefore, the absolute values cannot be used, since they certainly are much lower in the subvolume than in the whole lung. We only study the behavior of the relative values, computed in relation to the whole mass and volume of the subvolume. As an example, the relative mass of non-ventilated tissue for the whole lung is $m_{non_{total}} = m_{non}/m_{total}$. This is compared to the same value for a subvolume with a height of x cm, $m_{non_{x\ cm}} = m_{non_{x\ cm}}/m_{x\ cm}$.

The drawback of this approach is the uncertainty of the local relative values. The subvolume with a height of 2 cm usually contains only very few slices. It might thus happen that the relative qCT measurements are coincidentally similar to the whole lung, without being representative. We try to remedy this

	min	max	mean	median	std	unit
All: N = 159, Male = 116, Female = 43						
Age	14	91	41,1	41	17,20	y
Height	150	206	176	175	9,3	cm
Slices	18	67	36,8	31	13,2	#
ARDS: N = 89, Male = 61, Female = 28						
Age	15	82	46,2	45	16,40	y
Height	150	206	176	176	9,9	cm
Slices	18	67	40,3	44	13,3	#
Ventilated: N = 43, Male = 37, Female = 6						
Age	16	91	33,2	27	16,20	y
Height	164	195	177	175	7,7	cm
Slices	20	65	34,7	27	12,5	#
Spontaneous: N = 27, Male = 18, Female = 9						
Age	14	85	36,6	34	15,60	y
Height	156	193	174,3	175	10	cm
Slices	20	60	28,5	25	9,6	#

Table 7.3: Patient statistics for our study.

limitation by our large database of patients and the many qCT measurements.

The difference between the subvolumes and the whole lung is determined using Bland-Altman plots [15]. This technique is suitable for comparing two different methods, as well as for comparing a method to a gold standard, which in our case is the whole lung. The result of a Bland-Altman plot contains the mean difference of the two data sets (which is called bias), and a level of agreement (LOA), calculated as 1.96 times the standard deviation of the differences. On the vertical axis, the difference between the two data sets is displayed, while the horizontal axis either contains the gold standard data set, or the mean of the sum of the two data sets. Also, we use boxplots to visually summarize our results.

For the final comparison, an extensive literature search resulted in the finding that an error of up to 25 to 30% according to the following equation is acceptable for clinical research. Let d_1 and d_2 be two different data sets, for example the percentage of non-ventilated lung mass for all patients in the 2 cm subvolume and in the whole lung. Then the error is defined as

$$Error = \frac{std(d_1 - d_2)}{0.5 \cdot (\bar{d}_1 + \bar{d}_2)} \cdot 100\%. \tag{7.6}$$

Here, std is the standard deviation, and $\bar{d}_i$ is the mean.

Programming

Since all subvolumes (with total heights of 2, 4, 6, 8, 10 cm, named V_2, V_4, V_6, V_8, and V_{10}) were extracted manually and stored separately, our first goal is to reproduce the extraction automatically and to verify previous results. We detected several differences to the manual approach, which were discussed and corrected afterwards. Also, this allows our program to become as robust as possible since we could verify our automatic results. The code was then extended such that the extraction is performed on the fly without storing it on file.

For each CT scan, all DICOM files are loaded that also contain the segmentation of the lung boundary in polygonal representation. As above, the polygons are converted to a volume mask, and slice thickness and pixel spacing are extracted from the DICOM header. Thus, the volume of one voxel can easily be calculated. The CT slice closest to the fifth inter-costal space (named s_{ICR}) was determined manually beforehand for every data set. In general, it might be possible to compute this automatically, but still a thorough inspection would be necessary. Also, the values were already available from previous work. For the k-th subvolume of height h_k, the first and last slice are determined by

$$step_k = \left\lceil \frac{\frac{h_k}{2} \cdot 10}{st} \right\rceil, \tag{7.7}$$

$$slice_{start} = s_{ICR} - step_k, \tag{7.8}$$

$$slice_{end} = s_{ICR} + step_k \tag{7.9}$$

Here, st is the slice thickness, and $[\cdot]$ is the rounding operator.

The qCT measurements volume, mass, and gas content are calculated as absolute and relative values as described in Chapter 7.1 and stored in an

Excel sheet, structurally identical to the manually created one. The table comprises one row for each patient, while each of the columns contain one qCT measurement. The different subvolumes are horizontally stacked in one row.

Note that with this approach, we are able to calculate all necessary data for the analysis in one processing step, loading the DICOM files only once. Thus, we achieve a runtime of significantly less than one hour for all 159 patients, which is an enormous advancement in comparison to usual clinical studies where several weeks of cumbersome and error-prone manual work is required.

In clinical studies, professional statistical tools are typically used to analyze the data. Most of the time, many manual steps are necessary to input the data into the programs, and to generate visual results. To be more flexible in the early stages of analysis, and to generate results faster, we rely on Matlab programming. Here, many steps can be automated, and the data is available immediately, since the previous steps were also performed with Matlab.

Boxplots are used to display the distributions of qCT measurements for the different subvolumes, and to visually and quantitatively compare them to each other and to the whole lung. Relevant parameters, such as median, minimum, maximum, range, inter-quartile range, and whisker values, are stored in a table for comparison. Also, the boxplots are saved as vector graphics. Results are shown below.

For each qCT measurement, a graphical representation of the difference of each subvolume to the whole lung is computed using Bland-Altman plots. Furthermore, each subvolume is compared to its predecessor in terms of covered volume. In addition to the plots, the bias (the mean difference) and the level of agreement (LOA, 1.96 times the standard deviation of the differences) are stored in tables and aggregated in a summary plot, similar to Reske et al. [129].

As described above, the most common error function in the literature is applied to the data in order to quantify the difference of subvolumes compared to each other to the whole lung. These values are also stored in a table. All in all, several thousand highly reusable lines of Matlab code are developed, which make the collaborative analysis of the data much more flexible and significantly easier. Also, several different directions for analysis can be explored very easily.

Results and Comparison

The first step, verification of the previously manually extracted subvolumes and qCT measurements, resulted in several findings of differences. These were discussed with the medical collaborators to determine the source of error, which frequently was a slightly different slice selection due to rounding, or an error during manually extracting and copying the DICOM files. In summary, all differences between the manual and automated processing could be solved, resulting in a verified, trustworthy data collection.

While comparing the automatically calculated qCT measurements with the results from the *Luva* software, we made an interesting discovery. Our first version of the code used all voxels inside of the lung mask for the qCT measurements. In contrast, *Luva* only considered those lung voxels which are classified according to Table 7.1. This is the standard procedure. All other voxels inside the mask are discarded. As shown in Figure 7.6(a), the volume difference for many ARDS patients is significantly larger than 100 ml. It can therefore be concluded that the standard classification (truncating density values larger than +100 HU) can severely underestimate the true volume and mass of the lung. This is depicted in Figure 7.6(b), where the histogram excerpts for the HU range of -200 to +300 for all ARDS patients is shown. The red line indicates the cut-off value of +100 HU, while many voxels inside of the lung have significantly larger density values. A close inspection of the affected CT data sets revealed severe atelectasis or diffused contrast agents as the cause. Two examples are given in Figure 7.7. As discussed below, this has a potentially critical impact for quantitative CT analysis of patients with severe lung damage. However, to stay in accordance with the published literature, we continued our study with the standard voxel classification.

We calculated boxplots for all qCT measurements in order to visually and quantitatively assess the similarity of the subvolumes compared to each other and to the whole lung. In Figure 7.8(a)-(d), we show four different boxplots. The first one contains the absolute mass of the lung tissue in each subvolume compared to the whole lung mass. As expected, there is an almost linear increase in lung mass covered by the larger subvolumes. The remaining plots show the relative measurements for gas content (b), volume (c), and mass (d) of non-ventilated tissue. The similarity of all distributions can clearly be seen,

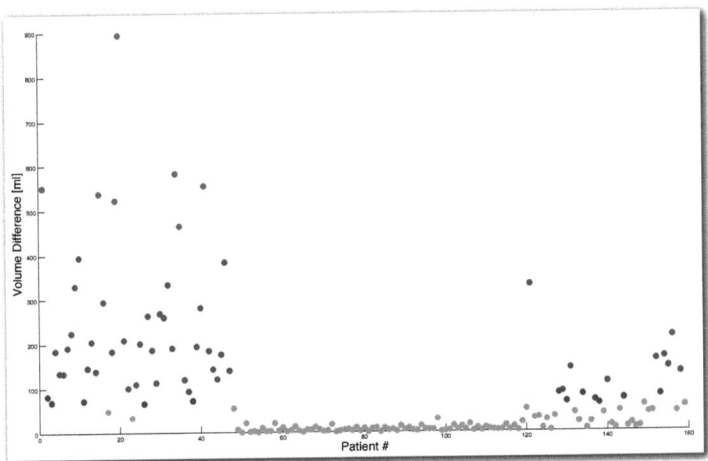

(a) Volume measurement differences with different voxel classifications. Purple and red values indicate significant variations, mostly in cases of ARDS patients.

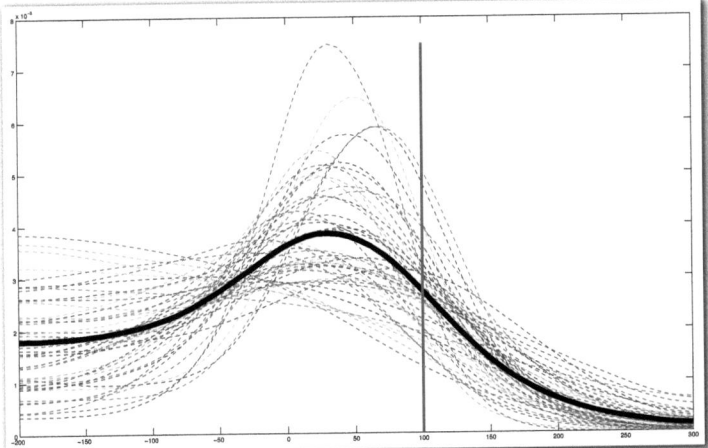

(b) Histogram excerpt for ARDS patients. The black curve is the averaged histogram, while the red line indicates the classification cut-off value of +100 HU.

Figure 7.6: The standard lung voxel classification can lead to severe underestimation of the lung mass and volume due to the cut-off value.

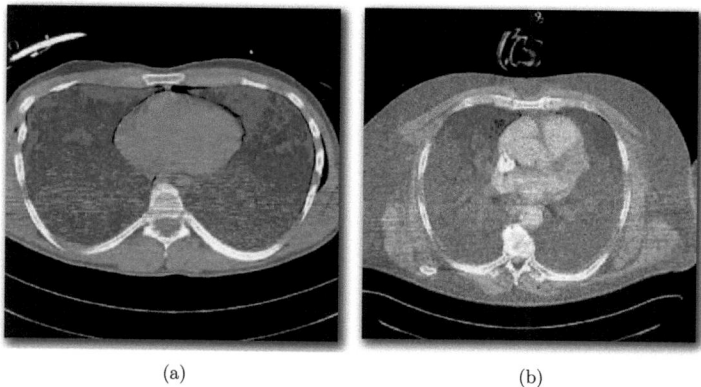

(a) (b)

Figure 7.7: Examples for mild (a) and severe (b) cases of misclassification due to the rigid Hounsfield thresholds. Unclassified lung tissue is highlighted in green.

indicating that all subvolumes are reasonably representative for the whole lung. The different parameters for these plots were also recorded, as can be seen in Table 7.4, which contains the numbers for Figure 7.8(d). In conclusion, we can already show that subvolumes of the lung around the fifth inter-costal space have a very similar distribution of qCT measures such as mass, volume, and gas content for all classified tissue types.

To determine which subvolume is sufficiently representative for the whole lung while also striving for a minimal volume size, we use Bland-Altman plots. They are automatically generated for each measurement, and for each patient group (all, ARDS, ventilated, and spontaneous breathing). Bias and level of agreement values are stored for each plot, and displayed in a summary plot. Here, results for the percentage of non-ventilated lung mass are presented, which is the most important qCT measurement as reported by our medical collaborators. In Figure 7.9(a), the summary plot containing bias and LOA values from all subvolumes of ARDS patients is shown. Apparently, there is no strong trend visible towards one subvolume, although the LOA curve's slope becomes smaller after the 4 cm subvolume V_4. This could indicate that the increase of volume does not justify the increased precision of the qCT measure-

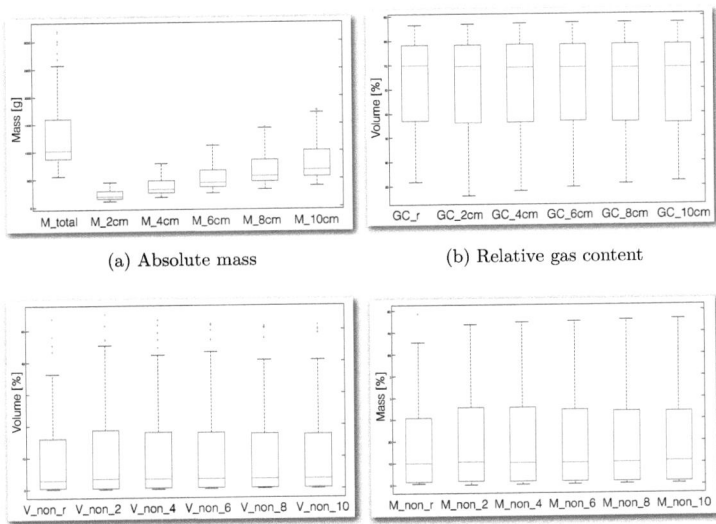

Figure 7.8: Box plots for all subvolumes indicating similar distributions compared to the whole lung.

ments compared to the whole lung for subvolumes larger than 4 cm or 6 cm. Figures 7.9(b)-(d) present the Bland-Altman plots for V_2, V_6, and V_{10} which correspond to the summary plot. Here, the difference of each subvolume to the whole lung is plotted on the vertical axis, while the whole lung measurements serve as gold standard on the horizontal axis. Note the large range of non-ventilated lung mass and the narrow LOA lines for larger subvolumes.

Since the comparison of the subvolumes with the whole lung shows first hints that V_4 or V_6 might be sufficiently representative, we also generate Bland-Altman plots comparing the subvolumes to each other in order to determine the best match. Here, the horizontal axis shows the average of both data sets instead of the gold standard. Figures 7.10(a)-(c) again display the summary plots for bias and LOA for the percentage of non-ventilated lung mass, but now each subvolume is compared to its predecessor. For each patient group, here all patients (a), ARDS patients (b), and spontaneously breathing patients

Parameter	M_{non_r} total	M_{non_r} 2 cm	M_{non_r} 6 cm	M_{non_r} 6 cm	M_{non_r} 8 cm	M_{non_r} 10 cm
Median	10,05	10,56	10,15	10,15	10,35	10,81
Minimum	0,54	0,03	0,08	0,29	0,43	0,61
Maximum	78,65	73,59	74,62	75,03	75,60	76,08
Range	78,11	73,56	74,54	74,74	75,16	75,47
1st Quartile	1,48	1,68	1,59	1,61	1,53	1,56
3rd Quartile	30,69	35,39	35,52	34,49	33,7	33,48
IQR	29,21	33,71	33,93	32,88	32,17	31,92
Whisker low	0,54	0,03	0,08	0,29	0,43	0,61
Whisker high	65,51	73,59	74,62	75,03	75,60	76,08

Table 7.4: Boxplot parameters for relative non-ventilated mass in [%].

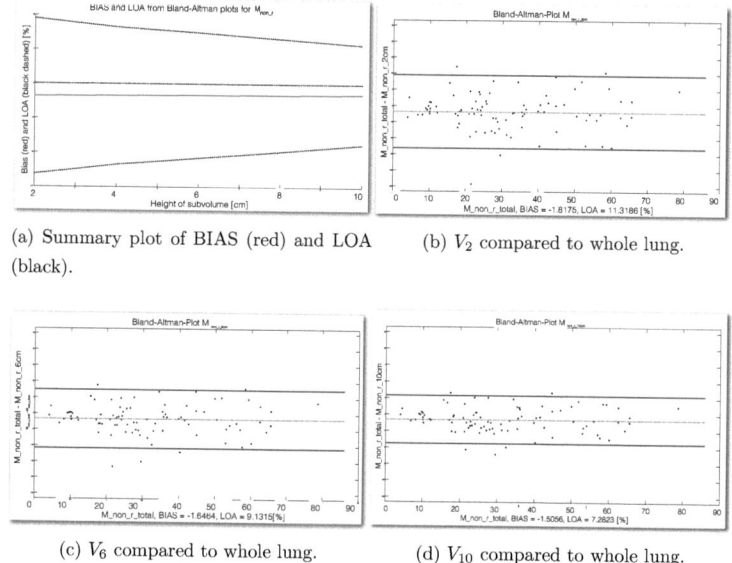

(a) Summary plot of BIAS (red) and LOA (black).

(b) V_2 compared to whole lung.

(c) V_6 compared to whole lung.

(d) V_{10} compared to whole lung.

Figure 7.9: Bland-Altman plots for relative non-ventilated mass of subvolumes compared to the whole lung.

(c), it is clearly visible that the difference of V_6 to V_4 is much larger than that of V_4 to V_2. For larger subvolumes, all curve slopes become again significantly smaller, meaning that the improvement from one subvolume to the next is not as large as its increase in size. Figure 7.10(d) is a Bland-Altman plot of the difference of V_6 to V_4 for ARDS patients.

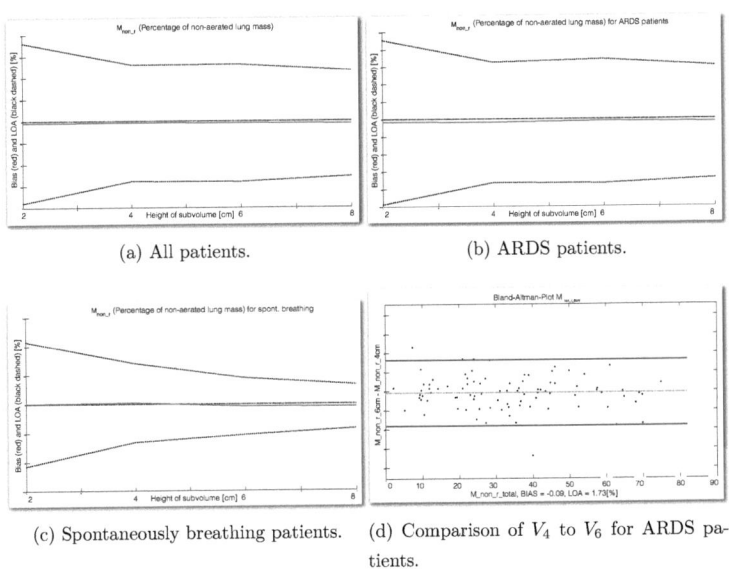

(a) All patients.

(b) ARDS patients.

(c) Spontaneously breathing patients.

(d) Comparison of V_4 to V_6 for ARDS patients.

Figure 7.10: Bland-Altman summary plots of BIAS (red) and LOA (black) for relative non-ventilated mass.

We summarize the bias and LOA values for all Bland-Altman plots of ARDS patients in Table 7.5, while Table 7.6 shows the results from the summary plot in Figure 7.10(b) and for all other measurements.

Note that the qCT measurements are given as percentage of the total volume or mass of the respective subvolume. Thus, the bias and LOA values are given in the same unit, but values for different measurements are not directly comparable.

In our final analysis step, we determine the error according to Equation 7.6, which is independent of the total measurement value of the specific subvolume.

Var.	V_2 BIAS / LOA	V_4 BIAS / LOA	V_6 BIAS / LOA	V_8 BIAS / LOA	V_{10} BIAS / LOA
V_{non_r}	-1,66 / 8,50	-1,56 / 7,56	-1,43 / 6,93	-1,31 / 6,11	-1,18 / 5,32
V_{poor_r}	-1,17 / 8,63	-1,03 / 8,09	-0,86 / 7,29	-0,79 / 6,40	-0,68 / 5,51
V_{norm_r}	2,43 / 12,24	2,16 / 11,34	1,94 / 10,32	1,85 / 9,00	1,67 / 7,75
V_{hyp_r}	0,40 / 3,75	0,42 / 3,45	0,35 / 3,09	0,26 / 2,80	0,19 / 2,48
GC_r	1,96 / 9,11	1,83 / 8,26	1,62 / 7,39	1,46 / 6,45	1,28 / 5,59
M_{non_r}	-1,82 / 11,32	-1,74 / 10,01	-1,65 / 9,13	-1,59 / 8,23	-1,51 / 7,28
M_{poor_r}	-0,70 / 8,25	-0,60 / 7,55	-0,45 / 6,66	-0,40 / 5,75	-0,32 / 4,91
M_{norm_r}	2,37 / 12,30	2,18 / 11,16	1,96 / 9,97	1,87 / 8,73	1,74 / 7,54

Table 7.5: Summary of BIAS and LOA values for ARDS patients, given in [%].

Var.	V_4 vs. V_2 BIAS / LOA	V_6 vs. V_4 BIAS / LOA	V_8 vs. V_6 BIAS / LOA	V_{10} vs. V_8 BIAS / LOA
V_{non_r}	-0,10 / 1,67	-0,13 / 1,26	-0,12 / 1,37	-0,13 / 1,25
V_{poor_r}	-0,14 / 1,54	-0,16 / 1,44	-0,07 / 1,42	-0,11 / 1,18
V_{norm_r}	0,27 / 2,17	0,22 / 2,01	0,09 / 2,12	0,18 / 1,84
V_{hyp_r}	-0,02 / 0,67	0,07 / 0,64	0,09 / 0,56	0,07 / 0,52
GC_r	0,13 / 1,70	0,21 / 1,54	0,16 / 1,53	0,18 / 1,29
M_{non_r}	-0,08 / 2,35	-0,09 / 1,73	-0,06 / 1,78	-0,08 / 1,61
M_{poor_r}	-0,10 / 1,81	-0,15 / 1,53	-0,05 / 1,39	-0,07 / 1,17
M_{norm_r}	0,19 / 2,51	0,22 / 2,13	0,08 / 1,95	0,13 / 1,75

Table 7.6: Comparison of BIAS and LOA for different subvolumes, given in [%].

These numbers are presented in Table 7.7 for the comparison of each subvolume to the whole lung, and in Table 7.8 for the comparison between subvolumes. Exemplarily, the errors for the percentage of non-ventilated mass (M_{non_r}) are plotted in Figures 7.11(a)-(b), for Table 7.7 and Table 7.8, respectively.

It can easily be seen that the error for comparisons to the whole lung decreases almost linearly. More interestingly, there is a large error drop for V_6 vs. V_4 compared to V_4 vs. V_2. For larger subvolumes, the comparison error

Variables	V_2	V_4	V_6	V_8	V_{10}
V_{non_r}	25,08	22,38	20,57	18,20	15,90
V_{poor_r}	19,62	18,45	16,69	14,67	12,67
V_{norm_r}	11,31	10,46	9,50	8,27	7,12
V_{hyp_r}	37,81	34,93	31,07	27,87	24,55
GC_r	8,91	8,07	7,20	6,28	5,43
M_{non_r}	17,67	15,65	14,30	12,90	11,43
M_{poor_r}	14,26	13,08	11,56	9,99	8,54
M_{norm_r}	17,07	15,44	13,76	12,03	10,38

Table 7.7: Error of subvolumes compared to the whole lung (ARDS patients), in [%].

Variables	V_4 vs. V_2	V_6 vs. V_4	V_8 vs. V_6	V_{10} vs. V_8
V_{non_r}	4,72	3,57	3,92	3,61
V_{poor_r}	3,43	3,23	3,20	2,67
V_{norm_r}	2,04	1,89	1,99	1,72
V_{hyp_r}	7,05	6,66	5,79	5,26
GC_r	1,69	1,52	1,51	1,27
M_{non_r}	3,58	2,63	2,71	2,47
M_{poor_r}	3,09	2,62	2,39	2,02
M_{norm_r}	3,59	3,04	2,76	2,47

Table 7.8: Error of subvolumes compared to each other (ARDS patients), in [%].

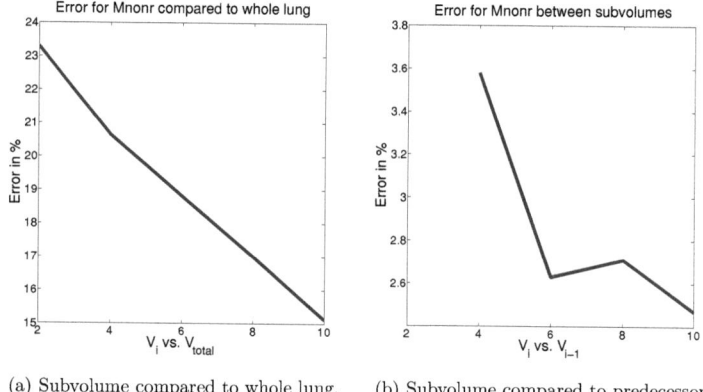

(a) Subvolume compared to whole lung. (b) Subvolume compared to predecessor.

Figure 7.11: Summary plot of the error of relative non-ventilated mass.

does not change significantly.

Conclusions

Our study found that most relative measurements for volume, mass and gas content of all subvolumes show a good correspondence to the whole lung. In terms of the Bland-Altman level of agreement parameter and the standard error measure, an almost linear improvement is observed when comparing the subvolumes to the whole lung. However, a more detailed analysis revealed that there is a drop in improvement after V_6 in almost all measurements. This is especially visible when comparing subvolumes to their predecessor, as shown in Figures 7.10 and 7.11(b).

The local statistics used in this study, notably the mass and volume of differently ventilated lung tissue compared to the total mass and volume of this subvolume, indicate that the measurement distributions are very similar to each other and to the whole lung, as depicted in Figures 7.8(b)-(d). Our report focuses mostly on the percentage of non-ventilated lung mass in ARDS patients, because it is the most important measurement for clinicians. Nevertheless, our study also includes more measurements and a broader range of patients. All phenomena reported here apply in a similar way to all patient groups.

There are several limitations of our approach. In many patients with lung damage, especially ARDS patients, severe atelectasis and effusions are located in the lower dorsal lung regions due to gravity and the supine position. These regions can be missed by smaller subvolumes, which might result in a non-representative qCT measurement distribution. Conversely, our study could not confirm this concern, as shown for example in Figure 7.8(d). The second limitation concerns the reported problems with the standard density classification. As can be seen in Figure 7.7, the upper threshold of +100 HU for non-ventilated lung tissue can miss significant amounts of tissue of interest, especially in patients with very severe lung injury. Therefore, our results could be distorted for ARDS patients (compare Figure 7.6(a)). Unfortunately, this issue cannot be solved easily, since the density threshold is widely accepted in the literature and cannot be modified on short notice.

In summary, we can conclude that, as expected, a subvolume around the fifth inter-costal space with a height of 6 cm delivers the best trade-off between precision of relative qCT measurement and volume size among the studied subvolumes.

Impact and Future Work

First of all, we can report that due to the collaboration between a computer scientist and a medical expert, the data collection and analysis could be performed significantly faster than in previous projects. Also, using a programming environment such as Matlab for the statistical analysis and graphics generation allowed for much greater flexibility and more experimentation than more rigid professional analysis tools. This is due to the fact that the common tools are suited for usage by medical experts, but therefore lack flexibility.

We conclude from Chapters 7.1 and 7.2 that the collaboration between computer scientists and medical experts is very fruitful, and the benefit for both groups has been significant. Fast prototyping and experimental software development also allowed us to follow different directions during calculations and the analysis, which was prohibitively time-consuming in previous projects.

Since both the lung approximation with ten slices and the extraction of a 6 cm subvolume have been shown to be representative for the whole lung for qCT analysis, these approaches are also considered as 3D thorax models for EIT image reconstruction. This is detailed in Chapter 8.

As future work, we plan to integrate the extraction and analysis of subvolumes into our multi-purpose framework, which we outline in the next section. Also, we plan to improve the compatibility to professional statistical analysis tools, which are commonly used in the medical domain.

7.3 Development of a CT Segmentation Platform

Introduction

From our joint efforts as described in Chapters 4, 7.1, and 7.2, we concluded that a robust, reliable, and fast multi-purpose software platform is necessary to better bundle our efforts and be sustainable for long-term use. The current workflow of our medical collaborators is based on a variety of software tools, which are inflexible and often outdated. As we previously reported in this chapter, developing specifically tailored software is very fruitful for clinical research. However, the presented solutions cannot be generalized, are not sustainable, and are not very robust and intuitive to use.

Our vision is therefore to develop a multi-purpose platform that incorporates all of our workflows for segmentation, qCT analysis, CT atlas generation, and EIT model computation. Here, we report the setting and early works as well as our outline for future work.

Previous Work

The current software tools used by our collaborators are shortly described in the previous sections, especially *Osiris* for manual lung shape segmentation and *Luva* for qCT calculations (Figure 7.2). Their main drawbacks are their age, lack of stability and of flexibility. Other, more suitable multi-purpose frameworks were developed during the last years. These are more general than is required for our purpose, for example *3D Slicer* [56]. This software has very recently even been used for 2.5D EIT model generation and EIT image quality calculations [38].

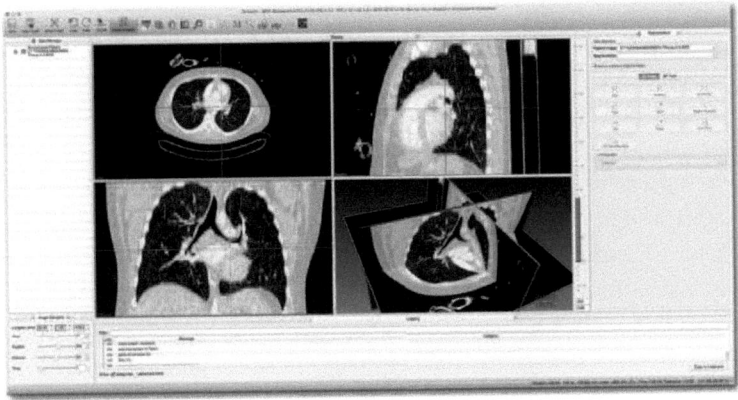

Figure 7.12: Screenshot of *MITK* showing a human thorax CT scan.

We decided to use the Medical Imaging Toolkit (*MITK*) as a basis for our framework [105, 115]. It is very general, in active development, and uses state-of-the-art libraries such as *Qt 5*, *VTK 6*, *ITK 4.5*, and others. Also, the plugin framework allows to easily develop and integrate own modules while exploiting the many built-in features like visualization, segmentation, and data structures. See Figure 7.12 for an example screenshot.

Data and Collaboration

It can be seen from the previous sections of this chapter that our medical collaborators have hundreds of CT scans available from both pigs and human patients. For many subjects, several scans were recorded, and many of them were previously segmented using a (mostly) manual workflow. Also, only the lung boundary is delineated, but for EIT model generation and CT atlas, it is critical to compute a multi-material segmentation including thorax, heart shape, and others.

In order to not lose all the valuable information in these data sets that were created in countless hours of cumbersome work, it is critical that our proposed framework is completely backwards compatible.

Requirements

The most important requirement for our framework is extraordinary usability by medical researchers. Many existing software solutions are designed towards visualization and image processing experts, but are commonly not very comprehensible and intuitive for clinical staff. In most cases, this is also the main reason that such tools are often rejected by those researchers. Additionally, a successful software needs to be fast, robust, and reliable, which in general does not hold for our current solutions. These are not in active development anymore. Therefore, there is no guarantee for them to work on modern systems, and there is no support for bugs. As mentioned before, the software is required to be fully compatible to existing data structures and formats. Also, it should feature at least the same functionality as the previous workflow in order to fully replace it.

Since we use both Windows and Mac operating systems, it is important to us that our framework is platform-independent. This can be achieved rather easily as many libraries and other software are already designed that way.

There is a general lack of and need for a sophisticated CT segmentation software. Therefore, we plan to release our framework as open-source to other research groups, and for future collaborations. The platform independence and the modular structure of *MITK* already support this.

In terms of functionality, the following requirements are crucial for our first version of this framework. We need to load and visually inspect possibly pre-segmented DICOM CT data sets. As shown below, there is a commonly accepted way to visualize this kind of DICOM data, navigate through the slices, and adapt the window on the Hounsfield scale.

The minimal requirement of a segmentation tool is to reproduce the current manual tracing of the lung boundary by a polyline. Additionally, region growing and intensity thresholding should be included. Currently, the lung masks are stored as polygons directly in the DICOM files. As this is an out-dated and non-standard approach, we should be able to only read those files, but we need a more standardized way to store the segmentation in the future. This becomes even more important for multi-material segmentations.

As we demonstrated in Chapters 7.1 and 7.2, lung approximation from ten slices as well as from subvolumes around the fifth inter-costal space can be used for qCT analysis instead of the whole lung. We need the possibility to easily extract the ten slices or the subvolumes, process them (segmentation and/or qCT quantification), and store them for future use. The link to the original data should be maintained.

We already showed that the qCT calculations can easily be performed without using *Luva*. This is also an important feature, together with the possibility to export results to Excel sheets and other formats for statistical analysis.

Finally, we hope to replace the current segmentation approach completely by our own semi-automated workflow as presented in Chapter 4. Also, we require a multi-material segmentation to generate EIT models, which is explicitly handled by our method. Naturally, this feature set is far from complete, and our framework needs to be flexible enough to allow the easy development and integration of future features.

First Results

We already reported first results of our own segmentation workflow in Chapter 4. It is demonstrated that it works in general, and produces multi-material segmentations in a convenient and potentially fast manner. However, our current Matlab-based implementation is too experimental and not yet suitable, reliable, and robust enough for use by medical researchers. Also, while the used algorithms have the potential to run very fast, our prototype is far from optimized and thus does not deliver satisfying execution times. However, we are confident that an efficient and parallelized C++ implementation as well as the integration of an intuitive user interface will render our workflow highly usable.

In a second step, we aim at developing a Matlab-based software that can replace the previously used *Osiris* for lung segmentation, integrating its most crucial features. In addition, our whole multi-material segmentation workflow should be integrated. Figure 7.13 shows the general user interface with manual editing of the lung contour enabled. The central widget displays axial, sagittal, and coronal slices of the CT data set, together with options to change the HU window and some presets. On the lower right, each of the segmentation masks such as thorax, lung, and heart shape can be selected to be displayed in the central view. Finally, the upper right view presents each phase of our workflow

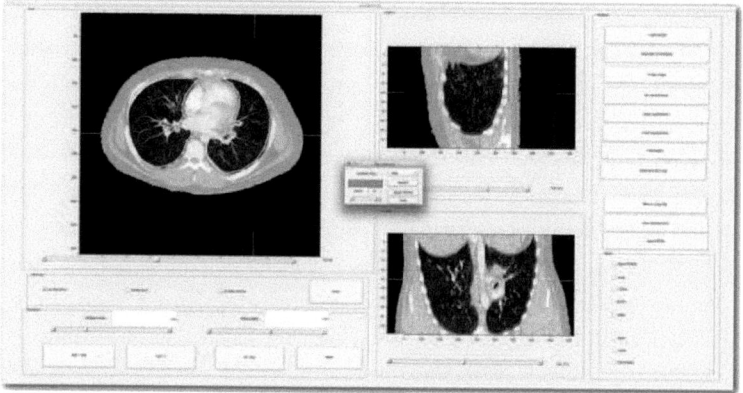

Figure 7.13: Screenshot of our Matlab software for semi-automatic segmentation. The dialog for manual lung contouring is active.

as a button, where the top-to-bottom direction represents the execution order. If necessary, a helper window is displayed for each phase, such as the one visible here for manual segmentation.

Although this software is functional, it is quite slow due to the Matlab implementation, and it is not robust and stable enough for longer use and batch-processing. Also, development of such sophisticated software rapidly becomes overwhelmingly difficult and complex. Thus, a more object-oriented and structured language would be more appropriate. Additionally, it is very difficult to integrate future components, and therefore, this approach is not suited for our long-term vision.

In conclusion, we decided to utilize a sophisticated, actively developed, and generalizable software framework, where many of the low-level processes such as visualization, navigation, and data I/O are already available.

First Experience with MITK

One particular framework that seems to fulfill all of our requirements is the Medical Imaging Toolkit, *MITK* [105, 115]. Our first experience with this software was very promising. It features great functionality, is platform independent, allows development of own modules to be integrated, and has a very active community. We were very quickly able to design and use our own modules, such as the extraction of ten slices or of a subvolume, as reported before.

Outlook

As the availability of such a promising multi-purpose tool is very crucial for a fast advancement of our research, the integration of all our previous efforts into *MITK* is our most important project for 2014. Step by step, we will replace our old workflows and tools, such as *Osiris* for segmentation and *Luva* for qCT analysis. Additionally, as mentioned before, our solution will be shared with other research groups. We expect our future workflows to be significantly more convenient and stable. The integration of our semi-automatic segmentation approach will reduce processing times from about six hours per data set to less than 30 minutes, while we aim to achieve a runtime of less than ten minutes in the future. Finally, a future project will enable the generation of EIT thorax models and the CT atlas using this platform.

Impact

A specifically tailored software platform for lung research (using both CT and EIT image data) is very unique in the medical domain. Thus, such development will be interesting to other research groups as well. We put a special focus on usability and interactivity, since these are usually not optimal for clinical use. Due to the possibility to easily add modules, we expect other groups to develop their own projects and integrate them into our tool, which in return is a specialization of the *MITK* framework.

The possibility of integrating other modules also fulfills our requirement for sustainability in terms of long-time use. We expect significant progress and faster advancement in lung research, EIT imaging, and qCT analysis due to the sophisticated design and multi-purpose functionality of this framework.

Chapter 8

Visual and Quantitative Comparison of EIT Models

This project was published as an abstract for a talk at the 15th International Conference on Biomedical Applications of Electrical Impedance Tomography in Gananoque, Canada in April 2014. A journal paper submission is pending.

We present a study to evaluate the anatomical precision of EIT images from different thorax models compared to reference CT data. A special focus consists of the patient-specific 3D models we proposed in this work. The research question is motivated in detail in Chapter 8.1. After presenting the data sets for this study in Chapter 8.2, we explain the model generation process for 2D, 2.5D and several 3D models in Chapter 8.3. Details and results for the image reconstruction are covered in Chapter 8.4, and the procedure for a quantitative comparison of lung overlap is demonstrated in Chapter 8.5. We present our results in Chapter 8.6 and conclude with a discussion and outline of future work (Chapter 8.7).

8.1 Research Question and Goal

The state of the art of clinical applications for Electrical Impedance Tomography is to use two-dimensional body models. These are generated from simple shapes like circles [33], generic thorax shapes gained from averaged patient data [152], or a 2.5D thorax shape gained from one individual [10, 57]. The only approach which is close to patient-specific models is a recent product by

Swisstom [17], where a set of pre-defined three-dimensional thorax shapes are stored on the device, and the model used for image reconstruction is selected on some patient-specific parameters.

In clinical research, 2D and 2.5D models are generated from one CT slice at the height of the electrode belt, while anatomical structures like the lung and heart shape are not always considered. The 2.5D model approach is the most recent research advancement, where the anatomical shape in the single CT slice is extruded along the vertical axis in both directions, assuming a vertical homogeneity of the thorax and lung shape. This assumption works moderately well for human body geometry, but is not very suitable for pig data, which are most common in animal experiments concerning lung treatment.

Even though the 2.5D model is an approximation of a three-dimensional shape, it usually overestimates the lung volume, while the heart shape might be over- or underestimated depending on the electrode belt position. Furthermore, pathological lung regions can occur at various locations and might be poorly modeled by this approach.

There is a general consensus in recent literature that patient-specific models are very important for EIT image quality and expressiveness [72]. Furthermore, three-dimensional shapes are assumed to be preferable to simpler models [3]. As this thesis aims to address these problems (confer Chapters 5 and 6), we are particularly interested in the visual and quantitative comparison of the effect of different thorax models on EIT images. As of today, there are no studies available comparing 2D, 2.5D, and 3D models with respect to their anatomical correspondence to real organ shapes. One recent study determines that organ shapes in EIT and CT correspond well when using a 2.5D model [57]. Their approach as well as their proposed equation for computing the overlap between EIT and CT shapes are currently unique in the literature and are the basis for our study.

We reported our first results generating patient-specific 3D models by a workflow which has the potential to be used in clinical research (confer Chapters 4, 5, 6). Still, these models require high computational effort, generate large amounts of data, and require the availability of suitable patient data. As reported in Chapter 7, our medical collaborators are interested in reducing the CT data needed to perform quantitative CT measurements. In this study, we compared 3D models generated from ten evenly-spaced CT slices as well as from a small subvolume of the lung around the electrode belt in order to determine whether these models are sufficient for EIT imaging. This would result in reduced manual and computational work, less data storage and less radiation exposure of the patient.

The main research question of our study concerns quantifying the (assumed) benefit of using 3D models compared to the current simpler models. As was reported before, assuming a homogeneous conductivity distribution inside the thorax severely influences the resulting EIT images [72]. Therefore, the conclusion is to account for the different conductivities of different organs like the lungs and the heart, which are most influential for thorax EIT. In this study, we quantify the effect of these complex models on EIT image quality and anatomical precision, and determine whether it rationalizes the larger effort needed to generate these models.

Although the state-of-the-art EIT images are two-dimensional, they show a lens-shaped projection (with a focus on the body center) of the three-dimensional conductivity changes into the plane formed by the electrodes. In the literature, EIT images are commonly compared to a single CT slice from the electrode belt level [57, 113]. Since we have a 3D segmentation of the thorax, lungs and heart shape available, we are able to compute a similar projection of this segmentation into the electrode plane. The aim is to investigate the suitability of these anatomical references for EIT image comparison.

If a patient-specific model is used which is obtained before the lung treatment, it is not clear how changes inside the lungs, of the electrode belt, or posture of the patient influence the EIT images. We intend to determine the effect of a time difference between recording of the thorax model and the EIT data.

Concerning these research questions, we formulated the following hypotheses:

- A three-dimensional subvolume with a height of 6 cm and a high complexity of organ shapes achieves the best overlap scores.

- The reference shape obtained from a projection of the 3D segmentation achieves a better overlap with EIT images than a single CT slice at the height of the electrode belt.

- Thorax models work best if they are temporarily close to the EIT data, i.e. the baseline CT delivers the best model for baseline EIT data, and the post-damage CT delivers best results for the EIT data recorded after the lung damage.

8.2 Utilized Data Sets

Although we have dozens of CT and EIT data sets from animal experiments with pigs available, we constrained the data for this study to one pig because of the high effort required to compute the dozens of different thorax models. As described in Chapter 3, CT scans during inspiration and expiration were recorded throughout the animal study. The first CT serves as baseline data before any intervention. Our second CT data set of the pig was recorded several hours later, after the induced lung injury. The pig already had a lung injury in the lower lung prior to any intervention. Confer also Chapter 9 for a discussion. The different lung properties before and after the injury are depicted in Figure 9.5.

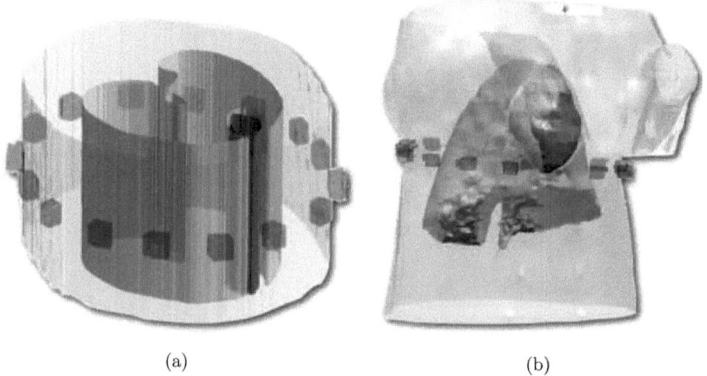

(a) (b)

Figure 8.1: 3D visualization of an extruded 2.5D (a) and full 3D (b) model with lung and heart shape.

We computed a multi-material segmentation semi-automatically for both data sets as described in Chapter 4, consisting of thorax shape, healthy and pathological lung, electrodes, heart, and major blood vessels in the thorax - aorta, vena cava and pulmonary arteries (see Figure 8.1(b)). Both the CT data and the segmentations have a spatial resolution of $512 \times 512 \times 118$ slices with 5 mm slice thickness.

We choose four typical EIT sequences for this study. The first was recorded during the baseline phase while the pig was mechanically ventilated with no spontaneous breathing. The second sequence shows the ventilation after the lung injury, while the third contains a lowflow maneuver with several reference breaths before and after the treatment. The fourth data set was recorded during a phase of apnea, where a saline bolus was injected into the heart after several seconds. Each EIT data set was recorded without any frequency filtering using a belt with 16 electrodes and the Dräger PulmoVista 500 device. 208 voltage measurements per second were recorded with a temporal resolution of 50 Hz. The reference data for relative EIT was manually selected as a short sequence at the beginning of each data set, while the time steps of complete expiration in these sequences were detected automatically (confer Chapter 6).

Figure 8.2 depicts the mean voltage measurements for each time step of each data set.

8.3 Model Generation

The input for all model generation steps consists of the three-dimensional, multi-material segmentations of the CT data sets (see Figure 8.1(b)). For each model type, the corresponding part of these segmentations is extracted, and the electrodes are modeled as realistically as possible for the specific situation, as described in the following.

2D Models

We choose three different types of two-dimensional models. The simplest one approximates the thorax shape by a circle with no interior structures. This model was used traditionally in theoretical and computational research on EIT image reconstruction. The electrodes are placed on the circle with equal

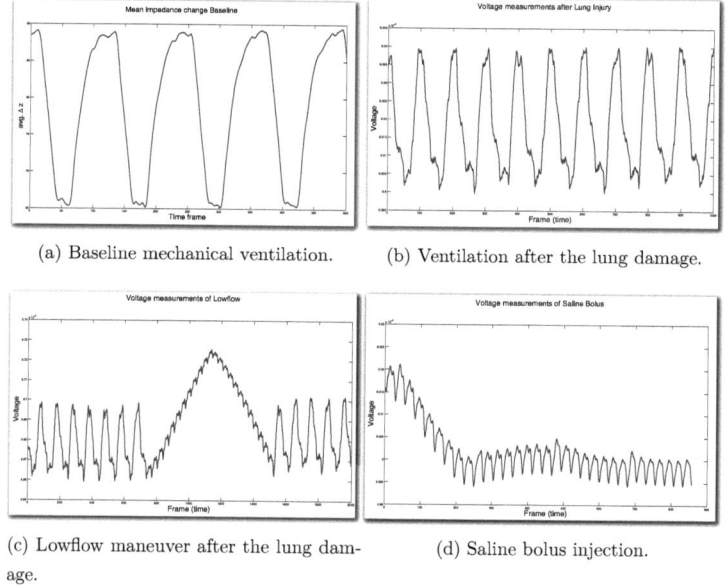

Figure 8.2: EIT data sets used in our study. Mean voltage measurements are plotted over time.

distance such that they roughly match the true electrode configuration. The second model is generated from a single CT slice at electrode level (Figure 8.4(b)). Due to anatomical restrictions, the electrode belt cannot be aligned in parallel. Thus we take the CT slice closest to the mean electrode height. Similarly, we extract the respective slice of the segmentation (Figure 8.3(a)). Our final 2D model consists of the projection of the 3D segmentation into the electrode plane (Figure 8.4(c)). This is done in a fashion similar to the projection of the whole thorax into the measurement plane during EIT recording. CT slices are weighted according to their distance to the plane (confer Figure 8.4 and [152]). For the CT-based models, the electrode shapes are determined according to the workflow described in Chapter 4, and then projected onto the thorax shape.

Although the EIDORS project contains methods to generate 2D finite ele-

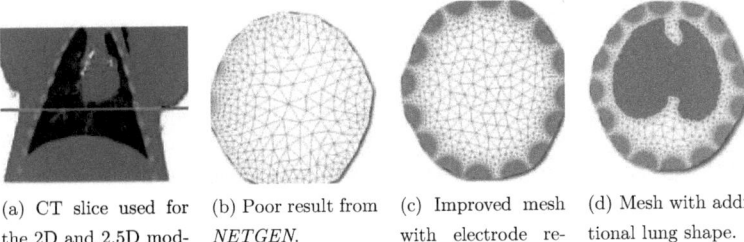

(a) CT slice used for the 2D and 2.5D models. (b) Poor result from NETGEN. (c) Improved mesh with electrode refinement. (d) Mesh with additional lung shape.

Figure 8.3: 2D model generation using `distmesh`.

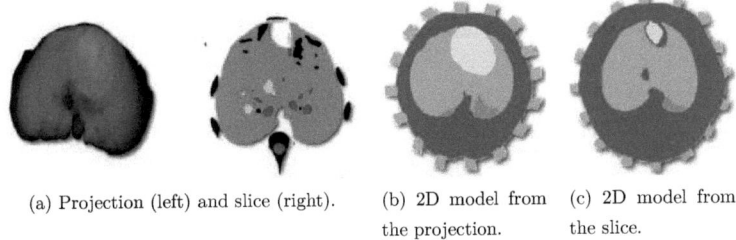

(a) Projection (left) and slice (right). (b) 2D model from the projection. (c) 2D model from the slice.

Figure 8.4: Comparison of a projection of the 3D segmentation into a plane and the corresponding slice.

ment meshes from curves, the results were not satisfactory. Especially the very important increased mesh density near the electrodes could not be achieved (see Figure 8.3(b)). Instead we use the `distmesh`[1] code to develop our own routines. Thorax shape and internal organs like the lungs and heart are modeled with a polygonal representation, while the high-density mesh around the electrodes is achieved by a circle centered at each electrode (see Figure 8.3(c-d)).

2.5D Models

The 2.5D models, similar to the 2D models, are created from both the CT slice and the weighted projection. Using *EIDORS* and *Netgen*, the segmentation

---

[1] http://persson.berkeley.edu/distmesh/

slice is extruded in both vertical directions, and converted into a tetrahedral mesh. The electrodes are reconstructed from the known shape and the position in the 2D model since they are not supposed to be extruded from top to bottom of the 2.5D model. Several more complex models could not be generated since *Netgen* is not very robust for those shapes such as complex pathologies and blood vessels. Results are depicted in Figure 8.1(a).

3D Models

The complete 3D models are created as described in Chapters 4 and 6. The first and last CT slices containing lung tissue mark the height of the volume, while the true electrode locations are kept. As shown in Chapter 4, the electrode shapes are reconstructed such that they match the thorax surface. The tetrahedral mesh is computed using *BioMesh 3D* as described in Chapter 5.

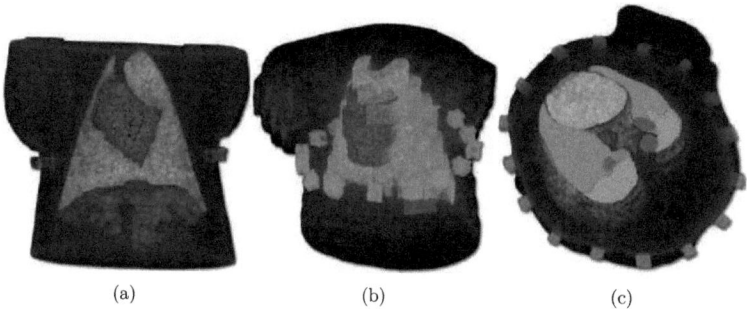

(a)   (b)   (c)

Figure 8.5: FEM meshes for a full 3D model with heart and lung shape (a), a 3D model from ten slices (b), and from a 6 cm subvolume with blood vessels and lung pathologies include (c).

A result for the full 3D model is presented in Figure 8.5(a).

Approximation with Ten Slices

As explained in Chapter 7.1, ten evenly spaced slices from the lung volume are representative for qCT measurements. Between the first and last slice containing lung tissue, eight slices are selected automatically (Figure 8.6(a)).

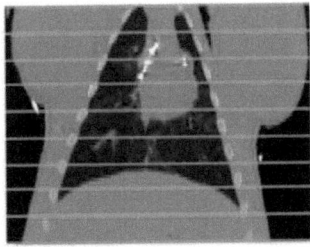 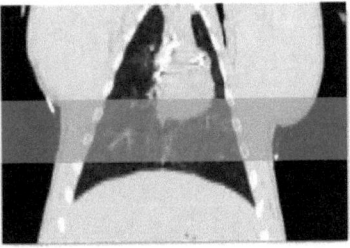

Figure 8.6: The ten slices for approximated lung models (left) and a 6 cm subvolume (right).

To fill the whole volume again, constant interpolation is used, resulting in 3D models as shown in Figure 8.5(b). Again, *BioMesh 3D* is used for meshing, as depicted in Figure 8.5(b).

Subvolume with 6 cm Height

Chapter 7.2 details our efforts to compare subvolumes of different heights around the electrode belt for their suitability for qCT calculations. Since our results indicate that a volume with a height of 6 cm gives a good trade-off between amount of data and precision of the qCT measurements, and since it is generally assumed that this volume has the most prominent effect on the EIT images, we chose these subvolumes for this study. Counting from the CT slice used for 2D and 2.5D models, all slices within 3 cm above and below this slice were included in the model, see Figure 8.6(b). The final mesh for the most complex subvolume model is shown in Figure 8.5(c).

8.4 Image Reconstruction

As described in detail in Chapter 6, we use the GREIT algorithm to reconstruct EIT images from the 2.5D and 3D models [3].

Since we are not able to use the GREIT algorithm for the 2D models, a simple Gauss-Newton algorithm is used (confer Chapter 2).

Different to the approach by Ferrario et al. [57], we use the algorithm by Deibele et al. [44] for the signal separation of ventilation and cardiac components of the final EIT images, as shown in Chapter 6.5. Eliminating the cardiac signal is very important for determining the lung shape in the EIT images, while it is also important to locate the heart and regions of pulmonary perfusion.

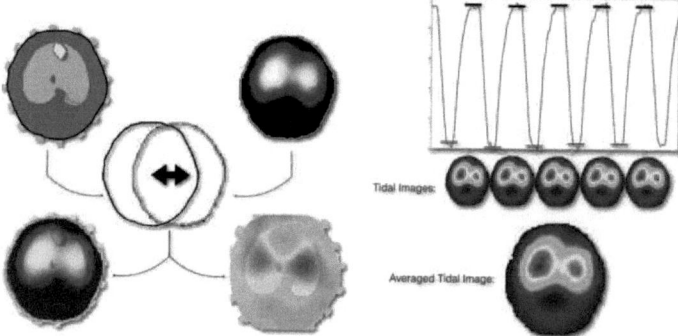

(a) Thorax shape registration and overlay between CT and EIT.

(b) Tidal images as difference between end of expiration and beginning of inspiration.

Figure 8.7: Thorax shape registration and tidal image calculation.

Due to differences in image size, resolution, and small perturbations, a registration is necessary to match the thorax shapes of both the EIT image and the CT reference image. As illustrated in Figure 8.7(a), we compute a linear transform to register the thorax shapes of EIT and CT images. While this approach does not accurately reflect the true perturbations happening during the EIT image reconstruction, we are at least able to gain a rough overlap of both data sets. Conversely, Ferrario et al. only upscaled the EIT images for comparison between EIT and CT without considering any shape deformations.

Typical EIT images overlaid onto the reference slice are presented in Figure 8.8. The top row contains results from the baseline data set, while the bottom row covers the lowflow maneuver after inducing the lung damage. Images from 2D models of low (a) and large (d) complexity, 2.5D models (b,e) and 3D subvolume (c,f) are given. The same order applies for the second row.

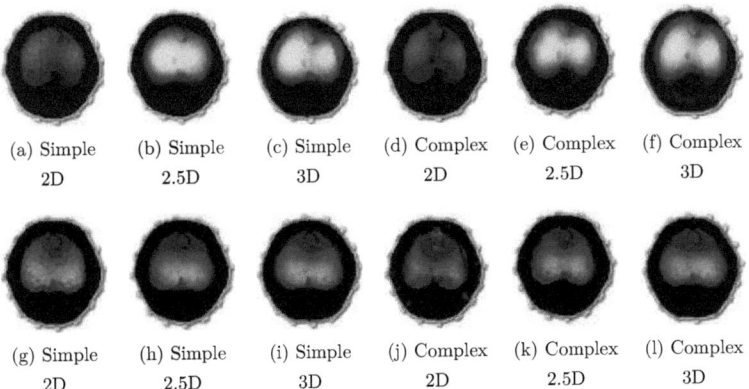

Figure 8.8: EIT results blended with the reference slice. Top row: Baseline EIT data, bottom row: Lowflow maneuver.

Perfusion images from the signal separation are presented in the top row of Figure 8.9(a-f), where the heart is emptied (blue) and the lung is clearly perfused with blood (red). In the bottom row (g-l), an example from the saline bolus injection is given, again showing the lung perfusion, but with larger contrast due to the large conductivity of the bolus. The ordering of the images is identical to those in Figure 8.8.

It is an open research question to determine the actual lung boundary from EIT images, especially in the presence of (mostly dorsal) pathologies. To compare the visual quality and lung shape overlap, we choose to use the tidal image. This is a functional representation of one breath, consisting of the difference image between expiration and inspiration.

We compute the tidal image for each breath and averaged over the whole sequence, resulting in a mean tidal image (see for example Figure 8.7(b)).

First visual results comparing 3D and 2.5D models were published by Salz et al. [138] and are also presented in Chapter 6.

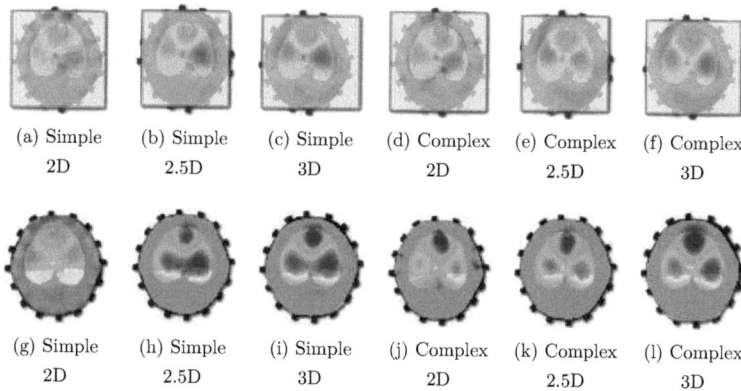

| (a) Simple 2D | (b) Simple 2.5D | (c) Simple 3D | (d) Complex 2D | (e) Complex 2.5D | (f) Complex 3D |

| (g) Simple 2D | (h) Simple 2.5D | (i) Simple 3D | (j) Complex 2D | (k) Complex 2.5D | (l) Complex 3D |

Figure 8.9: Perfusion images from signal separation (tow row) and the saline bolus injection (bottom row).

8.5 Quantitative Comparison

Due to the many differences between EIT and CT imagery, it is difficult to quantitatively assess the anatomical precision of EIT. First, EIT shows the lung function, i.e. conductivity changes over time rather than spatial anatomical information. Second, it is not a true tomography in the sense that an image represents a cut through a volume, but rather a lens-shaped projection of the three-dimensional conductivity change into the measurement plane. Finally, the very low resolution of 32×32 or 64×64 pixels compared to the 512×512 pixels in a CT slice produces severe artifacts like partial volume effects, and reduces the ability significantly to attribute EIT image structures to anatomical structures.

As of today, only one method has been published by Ferrario et al. [57] to quantitatively determine the overlap precision between an EIT image and a CT slice. Given a classification of EIT pixels corresponding to ventilation and a delineation of the lung boundary in the reference CT slice, the precision is computed as the fraction of EIT pixels overlapping with this true lung shape (see Equation 8.1, where $|\text{ROI}_{\text{Lung}}|$ is the number of EIT pixels contributing to the lung, and $|\text{ROI}_{\text{Lung}} \cap Lung|$ describes the number of EIT lung pixels that overlap with the reference shape *Lung*).

$$\text{precision} = \frac{|\text{ROI}_{\text{Lung}} \cap Lung|}{|\text{ROI}_{\text{Lung}}|} \qquad (8.1)$$

This is also done for the heart shape, which is calculated from the cardiac signal, as described below. This allows, as the authors conclude, for a determination of the rough correspondence of salient image parts in EIT to organ locations in CT data. However, the main drawback of this equation is the lack of consideration for the shape similarity between EIT and CT data. As explained in detail below, a thorax model resulting in rather small and fuzzy EIT shapes which are completely located inside the CT reference shape achieves a very high overlap score since the ratio of pixels inside and outside the lung is one. A more elaborated model with EIT lung and heart shapes that roughly match the true organ shapes, but lie partially outside of the reference shape (for example due to the low image resolution), achieves a poor overlap.

Ferrario et al. [57] perform a frequency-based signal separation of cardiac and ventilation parts of the EIT image, and determine a lung segmentation using a watershed algorithm. A tuning parameter for this algorithm allows to decrease the size of the pixel clusters that are supposed to contribute to the lung function. The authors compute these parameters, such that they achieve overlaps of 50%, 75%, and 90%, assuming that the larger the threshold, the higher the probability that the resulting EIT shape coincides with actual lung tissue.

Since we perform the signal separation using the method by Deibele et al. [44] and determine a functional EIT image from the averaged tidal images of several breaths, the watershed threshold parameter is not suitable for our data. Instead, we threshold the gray values of the tidal image to shrink the lung shape, resulting in an almost identical effect to the approach by Ferrario et al., see Figure 8.10.

We also reduce the shape until an overlap of 50%, 75% and 90% is achieved, assuming that the smaller the threshold necessary to reach a large overlap score is, the better is the used thorax model in terms of anatomical precision, at least according to the state-of-the-art equation.

To localize the heart and estimate its size in the EIT data, we use the output from the signal separation, which not only contains data from the heart, but

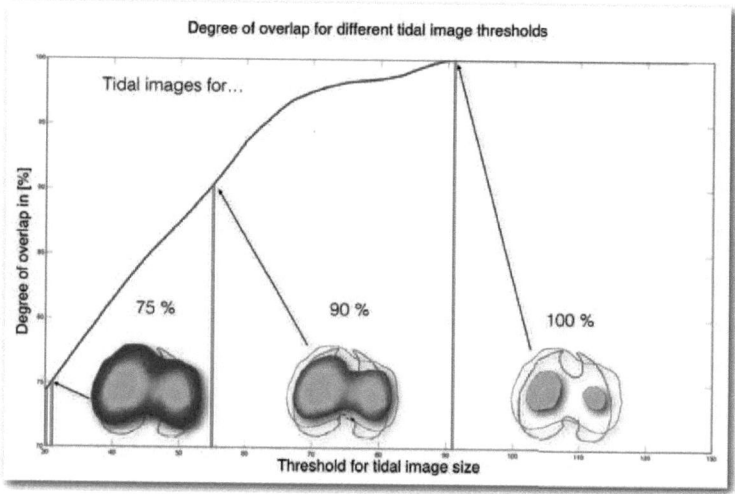

Figure 8.10: Thresholds and corresponding tidal images necessary to achieve an overlap of 75%, 90% and 100%.

also from pulmonary perfusion. Our approach is to localize the largest ventral (front) cluster of pixels with strong changes over time, since the heart region features the most prominent impedance changes. We start with computing the accumulated difference between time steps for each pixel using Equation 8.2, where $\Delta z(t)$ is the conductivity change at time step t.

$$\text{Summed difference between time steps: } \sum \|\Delta z(t+1) - \Delta z(t)\| \quad (8.2)$$

The result is depicted in the top left of Figure 8.11, with dark blue indicating very small changes, and red very large changes. This image is thresholded to only keep the relevant clusters of large changes. Furthermore, a distance transform is applied, resulting in the distance to the center of its corresponding connected component for each pixel. An automatic watershed segmentation is performed to separate the different clusters, and finally the largest ventral cluster of this set is determined. See Figure 8.11 for the whole algorithm.

After performing the signal separation and thorax shape registration, we determine the lung shape as the mean tidal image over all breaths in the EIT

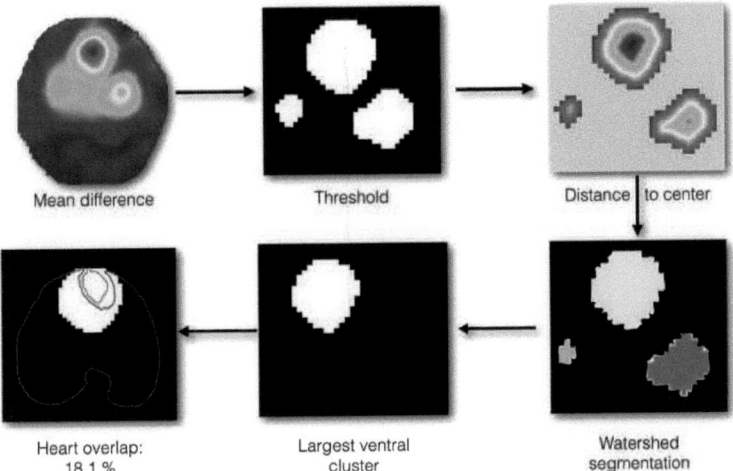

Figure 8.11: Heart localization from the accumulated difference image using clustering.

data set (Figure 8.7(b)). We calculate the overlap with the reference shape for each threshold value in the range of the tidal image. The specific thresholds required to reach an overlap of 50%, 75% and 90% are determined and stored for further analysis (see Figures 8.10 and 8.12). Note the different slopes of the overlap curves for the reference slice and projection, respectively. The slice results converge much faster to very large overlaps, indicating that the projection with its large heart shape is a worse reference due to the partial volume effect in "heart" pixels (confer Figure 8.4(a)).

Since we estimate the approximate heart shape in the EIT images directly, we only need to calculate the overlap for this shape without any thresholding (Figure 8.16(g-l)).

We perform the overlap computation for 53 different models (2D, 2.5D, 3D, 3D from ten slices, 3D from a 6 cm subvolume, each with varying complexities) and five EIT data sets (baseline, lung damage, lowflow maneuver, apnea and saline bolus injection). Overlaps are computed for both the CT slice and the projection as references. Due to this large amount of data, we only report the most significant results concerning our hypotheses.

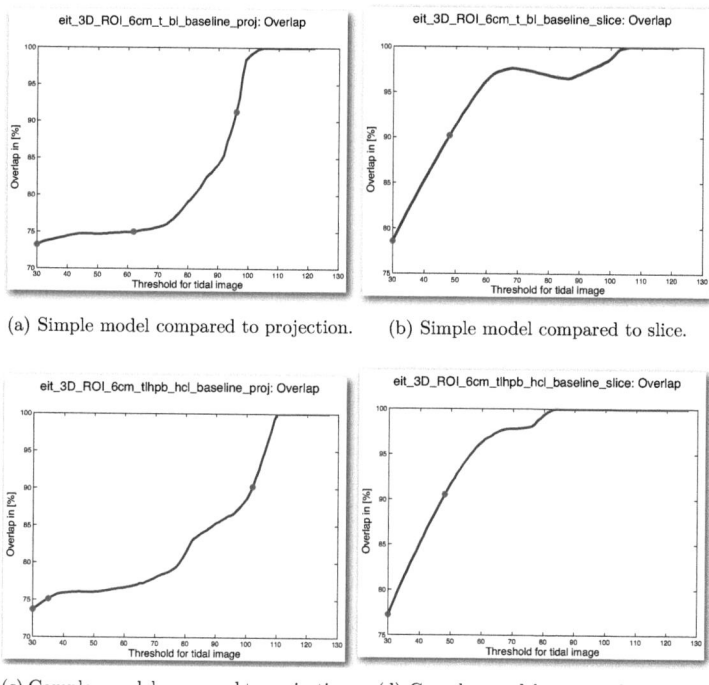

(a) Simple model compared to projection. (b) Simple model compared to slice.

(c) Complex model compared to projection. (d) Complex model compared to slice.

Figure 8.12: Overlap results for a simple (top row) and complex (bottom row) 3D subvolume model. Thresholds for an overlap of 50%, 75% and 90% are marked by red dots.

8.6 Results

We determine that the 6 cm subvolume scores the lowest thresholds for the tidal images to reach an overlap of 75% and 90% for the baseline and lung damage EIT data sets. Averaged over all data sets and complexities, the 2D models result in a mean threshold, i.e. size reduction, of 38.8% for a 75% overlap, 72.5% for a 90% overlap, and a mean heart overlap of 86.3% for the projection reference. The 6 cm subvolume yields a 33% and 88.3% threshold for 75% and 90% overlap, respectively, and heart overlap of 80.3%. If the slice is the reference shape, the 2.5D models perform slightly better on average than the subvolumes.

If we average over all data sets and model dimensions, we conclude that the models with thorax, lung, heart and pathology shapes are slightly better than those with thorax, lung and heart shape only for the projection. Similarly, the thorax/lung models and thorax/lung/heart/pathologies/blood vessels models receive results with insignificant differences for the slice reference.

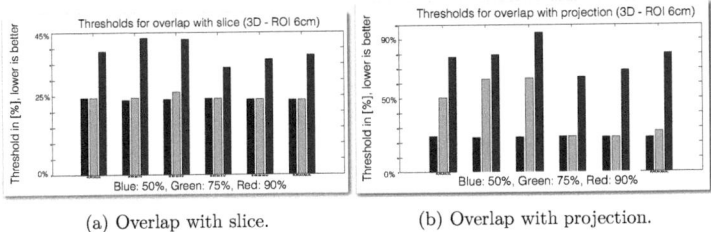

(a) Overlap with slice.   (b) Overlap with projection.

Figure 8.13: Summary plots for the 3D subvolume model. The model complexity increases from left to right. Thresholds for 50% overlap are marked by blue bars, for 75% by green bars and for 90% by red bars.

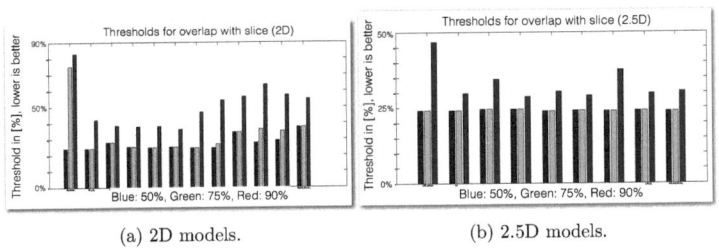

(a) 2D models.   (b) 2.5D models.

Figure 8.14: Summary plots for 2D and 2.5D models compared to the reference slice. The model complexity increases from left to right. Thresholds for 50% overlap are marked by blue bars, for 75% by green bars and for 90% by red bars.

These results are summarized in Table 8.1, while Figure 8.13 illustrates the difference between slice and projection references for the subvolume model. For comparison, the results for the 2D and 2.5D models are also given in Figure 8.14.

Model	75% Lung	90% Lung	Heart
2D (proj.)	38.8%	72.5%	86.3%
3D 6cm (proj.)	33%	88.3%	80.3%
2.5D (slice)	26.7%	41.5%	15.2%
3D 6cm (slice)	25.9%	50.5%	14.4%
tlhp[1] (proj.)	31.7%	77.7%	80.1%
tlh[2] (proj.)	34%	77.9%	82.3%
tl[3] (slice)	27.8%	49.9%	16.9%
tlhpb[4] (slice)	25.9%	49.9%	13.5%

Table 8.1: Tidal image thresholds and heart overlap for best performing models.

The mean thresholds alone are not very expressive for the true relationships in our results. We therefore analyze all models individually and in comparison to the others, and determine the frequency of cases in which the models are one of three best for a specific data set or complexity. Here, the 3D subvolume is slightly superior to 2.5D models, and more complex models perform better than simpler ones.

We determine a mean difference of 19.5% between the slice and projection reference shape with a difference of 8.2% for the 75% overlap, and 30.7% for the 90% overlap. Hence, we conclude that the slice achieves 90% overlap more often and significantly faster than the projection. The cause is illustrated in Figure 8.15. Since we binarize pixels in the projection, which contributed to both heart and lung, it features a much larger heart shape than the slice. Thus, EIT pixels outside this lung shape are penalized, although they are in fact in accordance with the expected projected lung shape (compare Figure 8.4(a), where the overlapping heart and lung pixels are colored in yellow).

To summarize the results for the lung overlap, we refer to Figure 8.16(a-f) which depicts the lung shape for simple (a-c) and complex (d-f) 2D, 2.5D and 3D models. Similarly, Figure 8.16(g-l) shows the heart overlap compared to the

---
[1] Thorax, lung, heart, pathologies
[2] Thorax, lung, heart
[3] Thorax, lung
[4] Thorax, lung, heart, pathologies, blood vessels

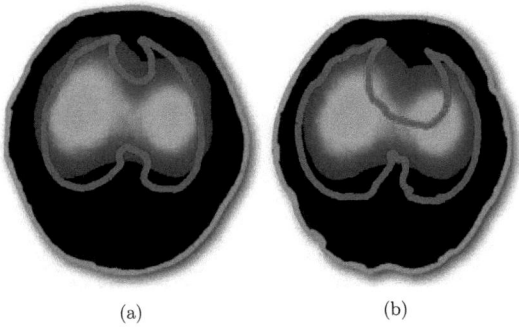

Figure 8.15: Comparison of the effect of using a reference slice (a) or projection (b) for overlap calculation.

reference slice. Apparently, the EIT heart shape is much larger than the CT shape. This is not very surprising, since the electrode belt and therefore also the reference slice are located quite low compared to the heart (see Figures 8.3(a) and 8.1(b)). However, the heart contributes more to the EIT image due to the projection. Typical overlap results of the heart with the slice are around 16%, while the projection reference achieves overlap of more than 80%, resulting in a mean difference of 66.7%.

Our results for the heart localization in the apnea, bolus and separated data sets indicate that the heart overlap is only 0.6% worse on average during apnea compared to the bolus. During normal ventilation, the overlap is 5% better than for the bolus. We can therefore conclude that neither the phase of apnea nor the saline bolus injection are necessary to estimate a decent heart shape in the EIT images. However, the question regarding lung perfusion or aorta detection is not considered in this study. Thus, further investigations are necessary to determine whether the bolus injection is clinically irrelevant.

8.7 Conclusion

Regarding our hypotheses, we can draw the following conclusions from our results. The 3D subvolume model with large anatomical complexity achieves the best overlap scores for most cases, although the margin to 2.5D and 2D

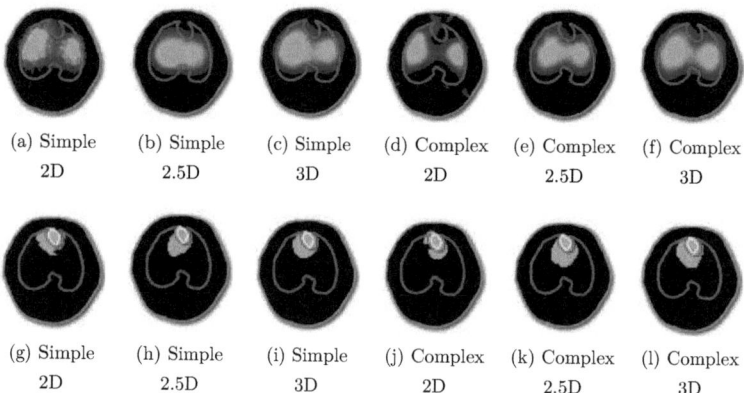

Figure 8.16: Visual comparison of the overlap of lung (top row) and heart (bottom row) for simple (a-c, g-i) and complex (d-f, j-l) models.

models is only small. This confirms our first hypothesis. The second hypothesis concerning the best reference shape needs to be rejected since the projection reference achieves significantly lower overlap scores for the lung than the slice. As noted above, this effect is reversed for the heart shape due to the mentioned reasons. Finally, although not covered here, our third hypothesis is confirmed: Models which are temporarily close to the respective EIT data set perform better than other, more distant models.

However, the most significant conclusion of our study is that the overlap calculation (Equation 8.1) by Ferrario et al. [57] is not suited for this kind of anatomical precision analysis. It only considers the EIT pixels which are located within the reference shape, without accounting for shape similarity or any other kind of correlation. Thus, as mentioned before, a very inaccurate lung shape such as depicted in Figure 8.16(b), which lies almost completely inside the lung, achieves a large overlap score. Conversely, a very precise, lung-shaped EIT image (Figure 8.16(f)) gets a lower score since some pixels lie outside the reference shape. Hence we derive from this equation that Figure 8.16(b) features a 'better' lung precision than Figure 8.16(f), although the latter matches the true lung shape more closely.

This motivates our future work, starting with the investigation of an overlap measure which reflects shape similarity and other parameters more accurately. A good starting point may be the research area of image similarity [158, 157, 43]. Also, Mamatjan et al. [106] propose a metric for data quality in EIT, which is not specifically tailored to anatomical precision. However, it might spawn future work regarding this issue.

Finally, a very recent publication by Crabb et al. [38] determines image quality of 3D EIT data by calculating mutual information between EIT and reference MRI. This is the most promising approach for our future work.

Chapter 9

3D Visualization of CT, EIT, and Segmentation Data

This chapter is based on a bachelor's thesis written by Gillmann [65]. My contribution to this work comprises the conception of the idea, specification of the tasks, and supervision and evaluation of the bachelor thesis. Additionally, the results were published by Gillmann and Salz with equal contributions [66].

In EIT-related clinical research, medical personnel, engineers, and computer scientists work together. Their research goals include technical, hardware-related issues, image reconstruction and processing, as well as applying EIT to clinical tasks such as ventilation monitoring. To bring the different backgrounds, working habits and views on problems together, a lot of interdisciplinary communication is necessary.

Not unexpectedly, researchers from the medical and from the visualization domain have very different views on the data, based on their education, their traditions, and also their practical workflows. For example, it is very common for medical staff to inspect three-dimensional CT scans slice by slice without additional visualization, except for the possibility to change the grayscale window to adjust brightness and contrast. On the other hand, visualization experts have been working on 3D visualizations of such data sets for decades, trying to convince domain experts of their improvements. Also, due to their mathematical background, computer scientists tend to interpret the gray values in medical data sets as scalar fields, which is helpful to select and develop suitable algorithms for image processing and visualization. In contrast, medical researchers see anatomical structures like organs and pathologies when inspecting the data, while mathematical properties are not of great importance. This is beginning to change with more intense research in quantitative CT (qCT) analysis.

Many discussions between computer scientists and physicians about methodology, results, and problems take place while looking at visual data. As there is currently no method to visualize the different data sets according to the medical researchers' needs, we aim at providing our own solution.

Chapter 9.1 describes our research question and the goal of the intended visualization. In Chapter 9.2, the data sets and their characteristics are shown. Chapter 9.3 is the central part of this chapter and details the utilized visualization techniques and design choices, while Chapter 9.4 gives some implementation details. Finally, we present the resulting visualization and how it addresses our research question in Chapter 9.5, and give a conclusion and an outlook to future work in Chapter 9.6.

9.1 Research Question and Goal

The state of the art of EIT visualization is twofold: CT data is viewed slice by slice. If present, the segmented lung boundary is highlighted. The only interaction consists of adapting the grayscale window to ranges of intersest. EIT data comprises two-dimensional images of the lens-shaped projection of the three-dimensional conductivity changes inside the thorax. The temporal resolution is usually large enough to view the images as a movie sequence. A standard colormap is applied, which highlights positive large changes in blue and white, small changes in dark blue to black, and negative changes (according to the baseline) in purple. No CT information is included into the EIT visualization due to the unknown anatomical correspondence of EIT image structures.

It is difficult for non-medical researchers to assess spatial characteristics of the CT data using 2D images only. Since medical researchers are trained to maintain a 3D mental model of the body while scrolling through the 2D slices, they show interest in 3D visualizations, especially in terms of visual communication. Also, it is difficult to compare EIT images with reference CT data for anatomical correspondences. This is due to obvious problems caused by side-by-side visualizations and the fact that the volume that contributes to the EIT image is much larger than can be shown by a single CT slice. Two examples that are difficult to assess solely by 2D visualization are the effect of the EIT measurement plane placement (depending on location and skew of the electrode belt), as well as the contribution of certain remote lung areas (below or above the electrode belt) and the heart to the EIT image.

Thus, our research objective for this project is the development of a 3D visualization of thorax and lung with an integrated view of EIT data to address these problems. The main challenges are to avoid cluttering (due to the large amount of data and occluding structures), and to provide an interactive application which allows free navigation and changes to the visualization in an intuitive way. What distinguishes our approach from previous work is the availability of a multi-material 3D segmentation of the CT data (compare Chapter 4), which enables us to exploit visualization techniques and design choices that are very rarely used in medical visualization.

Our goals are again twofold: We aim to improve the visual communication between visualization experts and medical researchers during discussions concerning collaborative research. Additionally, we intend to provide anatomical context for lung visualization, helping especially non-medical users to understand the imagery better. Some precise problems that we address concern the discussion of asymmetric effects in EIT images due to electrode belt skew, lung perfusion, especially in non-ventilated areas, and the influence of damaged lung tissue on the EIT image, notably the dorsal lung boundary, which is uncertain in the EIT images without further anatomical context.

9.2 Utilized Data Sets

Similar to the setting in Chapter 8, we used two CT scans of one pig wearing an electrode belt. One was recorded before an induced lung injury as a baseline, while the second one was taken several hours after the lung injury. The EIT data was also recorded after the lung injury. We used this particular data set to study the capabilities of our system and to highlight the difference between the true lung boundary (obscured by the pathological lung tissue) and the extent of conductivity changes corresponding to ventilation and lung perfusion in the EIT images. The images were reconstructed as detailed in Chapter 8, using a complex 3D model and registering the thorax shape between EIT and the CT reference slice.

A multi-material segmentation of both CT data sets comprising thorax shape, healthy and pathological lung, heart, electrodes, and major blood vessels was generated according to the workflow described in Chapter 4. Furthermore, each lung voxel can be classified based on the gray value (on the Hounsfield scale, HU) in terms of ventilation capabilities (compare Table 7.1). A graphical representation is depicted in Figure 7.4.

- -1000 to -901 HU: hyperventilated (blue)
- -900 to -501 HU: normally ventilated (yellow)
- -500 to -101 HU: poorly ventilated (orange)
- -100 to +100 HU: non-ventilated (purple)

Unfortunately, this classification is not unique to lung tissue, as most of the soft tissue in the thorax falls in the HU range of $[-300, +100]$. Thus, an inherent overlap of the histograms of lung tissue and other tissue occurs, which renders the development of a one-dimensional, grayscale-based transfer function highlighting the lung impossible. A volume rendering visualization of the CT data set, based only on such a transfer function, is depicted in Figure 9.1(a). It can easily be seen that the lung is almost completely occluded by surrounding tissue, and even voxels outside of the thorax corresponding to noise or clinical equipment is visible.

Since we have the multi-material segmentation available, the different structures can easily be separated, and specific visualization techniques, design choices, and transfer functions can be applied to each structure in order to achieve our visualization goals. This situation is very fortunate from a visualization point of view, since in most cases, such a segmentation is not available or very difficult to obtain. Only few works have dealt with visualizing this kind of data, as summarized below.

Finally, the severe challenges of the utilized data sets should be noted. First, the different data sets differ strongly in resolution: CT slices usually have a size of 512 × 512 pixels, corresponding to a pixel length of about 0.6 mm. EIT images only feature a resolution of 32 × 32 or up to 64 × 64 pixels, where the spatial resolution is about 20% of the thorax diameter. This causes significant partial volume effects and the effect of noise on the image data can be large. Furthermore, EIT data consists of many time steps with a temporal resolution of up to 50 Hz in contrast to static CT images. CT also suffers from noise and image errors, mostly caused by metal and other high-density materials, but also by a possibly large slice thickness, resulting in stepping artifacts.

9.3 Visualization Techniques and Design Choices

Related Work

We first present several related publications before detailing the design choices for the visualization task. Since we attempt to visualize multi-modal data from a CT scan, a multi-material segmentation, and time-dynamic two-dimensional EIT data, we studied similar approaches. Hadwiger et al. [78] are to our knowledge the first to implement volume visualization of segmentations on the GPU. Kim et al. [91] fuse CT and positron emission tomography (PET) into a single visualization. Salz and Reis [134] developed a fused GPU-based volume rendering of time-dynamic, three-dimensional microscopy data from multi-modal sources. Furthermore, surface rendering of additional data is available. Finally, Angelelli et al. [8] perform a registration and fused visualization of a 3D MRI scan and 2D ultrasound data.

One of the most important challenges for Volume Rendering is transfer function design. In the following we argue why common one-dimensional transfer functions (TF) as well as multi-dimensional TFs [95] are not well-suited for our task.

Another challenge when visualizing multiple data sets is the reduction of cluttering. Several Focus+Context approaches attempt to tackle this issue, for example Ropinski and Hinrichs [132] and Wang et al.[162] (Magic Volume Lens), Bruckner et al. [27] (illustrative Focus+Context) and Sikachev et al. [142] (dynamic Focus+Context).

Finally, Diepstraten et al. [47] use interactive cutaways for 3D visualization.

Since this project aims at the development of a preliminary prototype, we could not consider most of these promising approaches for our implementation. However, we discuss future work in Chapter 9.6.

Transfer Function Design

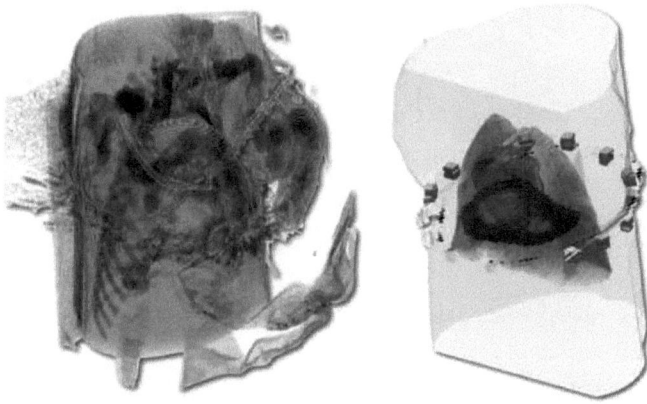

(a) Cluttered visualization using a global 1D transfer function of the standard lung classification.

(b) Our 3D visualization with a clipping plane at the front.

Figure 9.1: Images taken from [66]

A transfer function specifies a color and opacity value for each value of the data range. Gradient information [95] and curvature [94] might also contribute to the assignment. However, it is not possible to assign different colors and opacities to the same gray value depending on the spatial location or membership in a cluster or object. As mentioned before, lung voxels are classified based on their Hounsfield value, but other tissues in the thorax overlap with these ranges, as demonstrated in Figure 7.4. Applying this classification as a one-dimensional TF to a volume rendering of the thoracic CT scan of a pig results in the visualization presented in Figure 9.1(a). Apparently, tissues outside the lung severely clutter the object of interest. Since we have a multi-material segmentation of the thorax available, we are able to develop a

TF that not only takes image characteristics into account, but also the spatial location and classification of a voxel. Additionally, we can design several TFs for each material in the segmentation, irrelevant of their image features.

To reduce cluttering, we decided to only visualize the lung using Volume Rendering since it is the most important object of interest. Other structures such as the heart, the electrode belt, and the thorax boundary are only of interest for visualization experts as anatomical context. Medical experts already maintain this information in their mental picture. Hence, these objects are visualized as transparent boundary surfaces which do not clutter the view on the lungs.

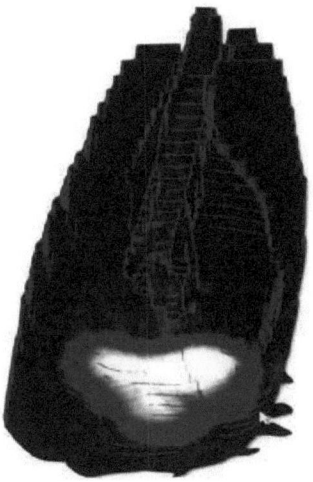

Figure 9.2: Visualization of the lung and EIT image with edge enhancement, taken from [65].

After excluding all non-lung voxels from the volume, we apply the classification shown in Figure 7.4 as a one-dimensional TF to the remaining lung voxels. Different opacity values are assigned for each class of tissue. The focus of our visualization lies on pathological, i.e. poorly or non-aerated lung tissue. Thus, these voxels get a higher opacity to highlight them in the visualization. Normally ventilated lung tissue is important for overall lung shape, so we assigned it a low opacity and additionally applied an edge enhancement to the boundary (confer Figure 9.2). Overdistended, i.e. hyper-ventilated, lung regions are also potentially interesting for this application, but we gave it a low opacity for now since we focus on the dorsal lung boundary and overall placement of the EIT reconstruction plane.

Embedding of the EIT Images

We can determine the exact EIT measurement plane from the electrodes in the segmentation. In some cases, the plane is slightly tilted due to anatomical constraints, as reported in Chapter 6. In Chapter 5, we set the reconstruction plane for such cases to the axial plane at the average electrode level. For anatomical correspondence, the time-dynamic EIT image sequence is embedded into our volume visualization at this plane. As described in Chapter 8, we perform a thorax registration between CT and EIT and upscale the much smaller EIT images.

Volume Clipping

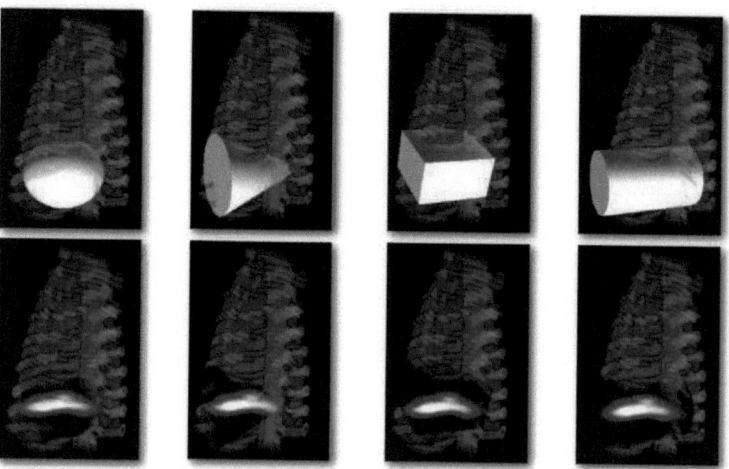

Figure 9.3: Different clipping volumes (top row) and the resulting visualization (bottom row), taken from [65].

In order to optionally remove some parts of the data in the visualization to reduce cluttering and focus on the region of interest, we implemented several volume clipping techniques. Entire material parts of the segmentation can be removed by selecting them in a GUI. Also, certain lung regions can be set to be invisible as determined from the lung classification. Clipping planes, as shown in Figure 9.1(b), remove all image parts in front of them. Thereby, several important context structures might be hidden, too. Thus, we implement clipping volumes, as presented for example by Weiskopf et al. [165]. These volumes can have almost arbitrary shape and allow an uncluttered view on the volume of interest, here the EIT image inside the lung, without removing too much context information. Confer Figure 9.3 for a visualization of several volume shapes.

9.4 Implementation

We require our software prototype to be fast, interactive and flexible. For this purpose, we chose the Visualization Library[1] as a framework, since it also allows for simultaneous volume rendering and surface visualization, and can be customized extensively. Figures 9.3 and 9.2 show early results from this implementation.

Although we met our goals regarding performance and interactivity, we were not satisfied with the visual quality. We therefore implemented a second prototype based on Matlab and the Vol3D framework[2]. As presented in the next section, visual quality is enhanced significantly. Unfortunately, frame rates are drastically decreased such that interactive inspection of the visualization is very difficult.

As outlined in Chapter 9.6, we plan to improve our prototype extensively and will also investigate an integration into the *MITK* framework (compare Chapters 7.3 and 10.1.

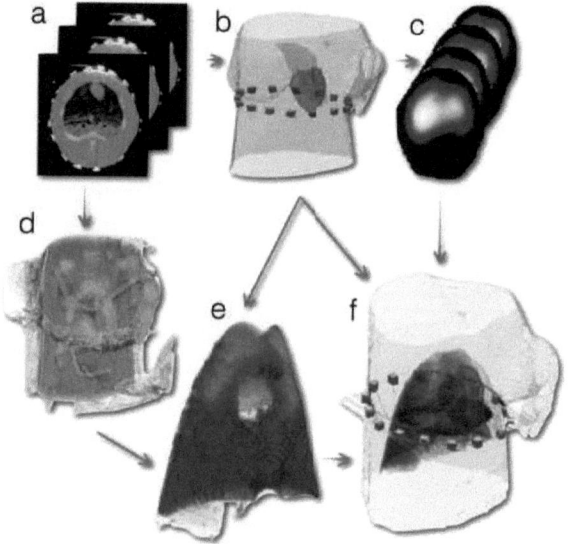

Figure 9.4: Our visualization workflow. Taken from [66].

9.5 Results

Our visualization workflow is outlined in Figure 9.4. In Figures 9.2 and 9.3, we present early results from our first implementation, highlighting the edge enhancement of the lung and volume clipping.

The revised visualization is shown in Figure 9.5 for both pig data sets. To the left, the baseline data is depicted. It includes the prior lung injury in the lower lung, highlighted in purple. Confer Chapter 6.3 for more details on this particular case. The same pig several hours after the induced lung damage is presented on the right.

With this visualization, it is easy to grasp the extent of the atelectasis (purple), the influence of the heart (red) on the EIT image, and the placement of the electrode belt in terms of contributing thorax regions.

As we reported in Chapter 6, the dorsal lung boundary in the presence of

---

[1]http://www.visualizationlibrary.org
[2]http://www.mathworks.com/matlabcentral/fileexchange/22940-vol3d-v2

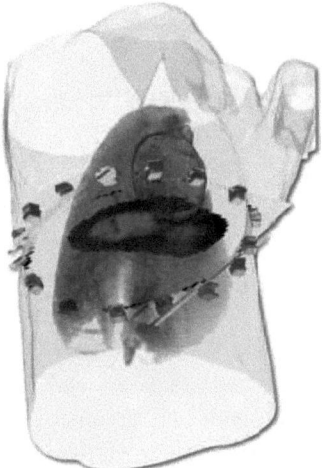 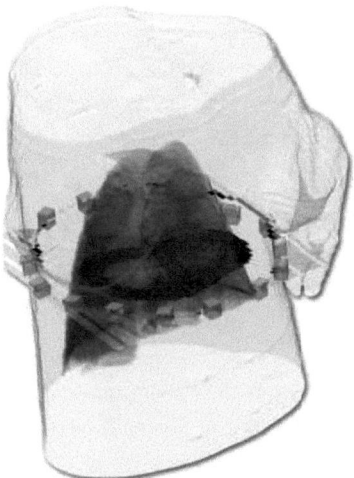

(a) Pig before the induced lung damage with prior injury (purple). (b) Pig after the lung damage with extended dorsal atelectasis (purple).

Figure 9.5: Results of our visualization, showing a volume rendering of the lung with pathological tissue colored in purple, boundary surfaces of the heart and thorax, and the embedded EIT image. Taken from [66].

atelectasis is of critical interest to medical experts, but it is almost impossible to be determined from the EIT images without additional anatomical context. We present a fused two-dimensional visualization of EIT data and the projected CT segmentation in Chapters 6 and 8, but clearly some 3D information is lost. With our volume visualization, the distribution of damaged lung regions compared to the EIT measurement plane can be visually assessed in 3D.

The main contribution of our visualization consists of an improved visual communication between computer scientists and medical experts during their collaboration. We presented several insights and findings from EIT data reconstructed with our 3D thorax models in Chapter 6.3. The discussions and visual verification regarding these insights proved to be lengthy and difficult due to the different backgrounds and visualization habits. Thus, the need for an accessible and interactive combined 3D visualization of the contributing data sets was identified.

As demonstrated in this chapter, we succeeded in providing such a multimodal and multi-technique visualization, and we conclude that our discussions regarding the results from Chapter 6.3 would have been easier and shorter with this visualization available. We hope to integrate these results into our future collaboration focusing on clinical research.

9.6 Future Work

The presented visualization is an early prototype, and many state-of-the-art techniques for improved visual quality and interactive exploration could not be included. However, we plan to integrate several methods in future work, such as curvature-based TFs for boundary highlighting [94] and illustrative Volume Rendering based on style TFs for context visualization [26]. As presented by Rautek et al. [126], interesting illustrative visualizations can be achieved by semantic layers. Csébfalvi et al. [40] provide high-quality volume rendering results for medical visualization using illumination-driven opacity modulation.

As cluttering is an important challenge for multi-modal volume visualization, transparency optimization such as presented by Chan et al. [30] will be investigated. Finally, the dynamic Focus+Context approach by Sikachev et al. [142] might eliminate the need for volume clipping.

Chapter 10

Future Work and Conclusion

10.1 Future Work

Introduction

While many research areas and problems are addressed, the main focus of this thesis is the development of a workflow for the clinically relevant generation of 3D thorax models for Electrical Impedance Tomography. We demonstrate the general feasibility of our workflow and develop several prototypes for the different steps, like CT segmentation, mesh generation, and qCT analysis.

Our future work will focus on details of the different steps, making them usable in clinical research. Furthermore, the area of landmark detection and image registration is only shortly investigated in this thesis, but will be a major project in the future.

Our first results for a multi-modal 3D visualization of combined CT, segmentation, and EIT data show a potential for use in clinical research by improving visual communication between medical experts and computer science researchers. Therefore, we will continue our efforts to develop a fully interactive visualization tool with high visual quality and state-of-the-art visualization methods.

Semi-automatic Segmentation Workflow

In Chapter 4, we describe our efforts concerning CT segmentation of the thorax. We demonstrate the general design of our workflow for multi-material 3D segmentations which has the potential to run in an interactive way with minimal, but intended user interaction. A prototype implementation is presented along with first results.

Our next efforts will include the implementation of a fast and easy to use software with focus on adding and removing sketches in almost real-time. In this way, it can be used in clinical research and the benefit of our method can be evaluated. An evaluation with medical users will cover the time required to produce a satisfactory segmentation result compared to the current (almost) manual approach. Also, the usability of our tool will be evaluated in a user study.

Additionally, we will investigate an integration into the multi-purpose framework based on MITK, as detailed below.

Mesh Generation

As shortly outlined in Chapter 5.4, the *BioMesh 3D* software produces satisfying tetrahedral meshes, but run time and mesh density are two factors that we plan to optimize. A collaboration with the SCI Institute in Salt Lake City, USA, will result in an integration of a GPU port of the most time-consuming meshing step with a speed-up of up to 20 times. Also, we will investigate an integration of the different steps and tools needed to produce a mesh into a single, easy-to-use workflow.

Finally, a future project will be concerned with mesh reduction such that the tetrahedra density is significantly lowered in homogeneous areas, while specific constraints can be defined, e.g. mesh refinement near the electrodes.

EIDORS and GREIT

The *EIDORS* code for GREIT training is very slow for complex 3D meshes and also has a very large memory overhead. We intend to optimize this code using better memory strategies, parallelization, and GPU programming in order to generate forward and inverse models from 3D meshes more quickly.

Furthermore, we develop a lot of improvements and extensions to the *EIDORS* software. These include 2D and 3D model generation, image reconstruction, signal separation, and more, which we plan to contribute to the

EIDORS project as soon as possible.

As reported by Zhao et al. [176], the *GREIT* algorithm is sensitive to conductivity targets near the thorax boundary. We will investigate this effect using our results.

EIT Image Interpretation

We intend to significantly increase our efforts in EIT image interpretation. As mentioned in Chapter 6, we will study the impact of our patient-specific 3D models on several published parameters and methods, such as pneumothorax detection and quantification of recruitable lung tissue. Furthermore, the first attempts of EIT image segmentation [75, 68] will be studied and extended. Rahman et al. [125] recently proposed to use Independent Component Analysis (ICA) for signal preparation of ventilation and perfusion.

We plan to investigate a novel and expressive similarity measure for the overlap between EIT and CT data as described in Chapter 8. Crabb et al. [38] recently published an image quality measure for 3D EIT imaging based on mutual information. This work is a good starting point for our future research.

EIT Image Registration and Landmark Detection

In Chapter 6.6, we describe our preliminary work and ideas on landmark detection in EIT sequences and image registration between CT and EIT data, for example the registration of thorax shapes for a reliable overlay of the different images. This project will be extended significantly in the future. Our results from Chapter 8 indicate very good perfusion detection during mechanical ventilation, even with the use of a saline bolus during apnea. Our major focus will be on the localization of the descending aorta as an invariant landmark for the dorsal lung boundary, even in the presence of severe pathology. While previous results were published using ECG-gating and saline bolus injection, we hope to locate the aorta and study the lung perfusion from signal separation alone, without the need of these additional techniques.

Once we can reliably and automatically locate anatomical landmarks in the EIT images, we will study the possibility of registering them with corresponding CT data in order to increase the anatomical significance of EIT and to investigate the effects of distortion and uncertainties during image reconstruction.

MITK-based Segmentation

In Chapter 7.3, we describe our first efforts in implementing a segmentation tool including many different processing steps such that EIT model generation and qCT calculations can be performed using a single software and standardized file formats. MITK has the potential to serve as a basis for such a multi-purpose framework due to its active development, modular structure, and the ease to add own modules. Our first step will be to integrate the classic, almost manual segmentation method which is currently in use, such that medical users can work in a fast, reliable, and user-friendly way. Also, data storage and handling of hundreds or even thousands of CT data sets is an important issue which will be addressed in the future.

We develop experimental code for the extraction of ten CT slices and variable subvolumes around the electrode belt from CT data, as well as for the calculation of qCT measurements and analysis. Preliminary work on integrating these projects into MITK are promising and will be extended.

As mentioned above, our own multi-material workflow will be integrated into MITK to allow for a fast and precise segmentation of the whole thorax, including many different materials in addition to the lung shape.

Finally, we will investigate the possibility to interactively develop 3D thorax models for mesh generation.

3D Visualization of CT, Segmentation and EIT

Our 3D visualization of multi-modal data, comprising a CT scan, a multi-material segmentation, and an EIT image sequence, will be improved in terms of visual quality, interaction, and state-of-the-art volume visualization techniques.

Transfer function design based on a segmentation is not very well covered in the literature, so this will be an important focus of our future work. Additionally, illustrative volume rendering for anatomical context, curvature-based transfer functions and other modern techniques will be investigated.

10.2 Conclusion

In this thesis, we present a detailed workflow to generate patient-specific 3D thorax model to improve Electrical Impedance Tomography imaging of the lung. This workflow consists mainly of a novel method to produce multi-material segmentations of CT data interactively, which has the potential to be used in clinical research. Furthermore, we demonstrate how high-quality tetrahedral meshes can be computed from a segmentation, and provide forward and inverse models for EIT image reconstruction.

A study comparing the anatomical precision of our EIT images from 3D models and other state-of-the-art models to reference CT data has twofold results. First, we conclude that our 3D models are slightly superior to other models in terms of lung and heart overlap with CT shapes. Second, we determine that the current method to calculate this overlap delivers unsatisfying results regarding shape similarity and general anatomical precision.

In addition to the proposed workflow, we report the results of two smaller projects in collaboration with medical experts to study quantitative CT measurements for lung research. For these projects, we develop prototype software which greatly accelerates and simplifies data generation and analysis, thus advancing clinical research significantly.

Finally, we present a 3D visualization of multi-modal data from CT, segmentation, and EIT, demonstrating how multi-material segmentation can be used to improve transfer function design for volume rendering. Also, the three-dimensional extent and contribution of lung pathologies and the heart to EIT images can be grasped easier when compared to conventional 2D visualizations.

We conclude that our work paves the way towards individualized EIT imaging with improved anatomical precision and more expressive quantitative measurements. Our results are expected to increase clinical usefulness and applicability of EIT, which will result in improved patient treatment and diagnosis. Furthermore, we demonstrate how a productive and successful collaboration between computer scientists and medical researchers advances and accelerates clinical research and raises new and challenging research questions regarding medical visualization.

Bibliography

[1] BioMesh3D: Quality Mesh Generator for Biomedical Applications. Scientific Computing and Imaging Institute (SCI).

[2] A. Adler, M. B. Amato, J. H. Arnold, R. Bayford, M. Bodenstein, S. H. Böhm, B. H. Brown, I. Frerichs, O. Stenqvist, N. Weiler, and G. H. Wolf. Whither Lung EIT: Where are we, where do we want to go and what do we need to get there? *Physiol. Meas.*, 33:679–694, 2012.

[3] A. Adler, J. H. Arnold, R. Bayford, A. Borsic, B. Brown, P. Dixon, T. J. C. Faes, I. Frerichs, H. Gagnon, Y. Gärber, B. Grychtol, G. Hahn, W. R. B. Lionheart, A. Malik, R. P. Patterson, J. Stocks, A. Tizzard, N. Weiler, and G. K. Wolf. GREIT: a unified approach to 2D linear EIT reconstruction of lung images. *Physiol. Meas.*, 30(6):S35–S55, 2009.

[4] A. Adler, P. O. Gaggero, and Y. Maimaitijiang. Adjacent stimulation and measurement patterns considered harmful. *Physiol. Meas.*, 32:731–744, 2011.

[5] A. Adler and W. R. B. Lionheart. Uses and abuses of EIDORS: an extensible software base for EIT. *Physiol. Meas.*, 27:S25–S42, 2006.

[6] A. Adler and W. R. B. Lionheart. Minimizing EIT image artefacts from mesh variability in finite element models. *Physiol. Meas.*, 32:823–834, 2011.

[7] S. Andrews, G. Hamarneh, and A. Saad. Fast Random Walker with Priors Using Precomputation for Interactive Medical Image Segmentation. *Med. Image. Comput. Comput. Assist. Interv.*, 13(3):9–16, 2010.

[8] P. Angelelli, I. Viola, K. Nylund, O. H. Gilja, and H. Hauser. Guided Visualization of Ultrasound Image Sequences. In *Proc. of EG Workshop Visual Comput. Biol. & Med. (VCBM)*, pages 125–132, 2010.

[9] J. A. Bærentzen. On the implementation of fast marching methods for 3D lattices. Technical report, The Technical University of Denmark, 2001.

[10] N. Bahrani and A. Adler. 2.5D Finite Element Method for Electrical Impedance Tomography considering the Complete Electrode Model. In *Proc. IEEE Canad. Conf. Electr. & Comp. Eng.*, volume 25, pages 1–6, 2012.

[11] X. Bai and G. Sapiro. Geodesic Matting: A Framework for Fast Interactive Image and Video Segmentation and Matting. *Int. J. Comput. Vision*, 82(2):113–132, 2009.

[12] D. C. Barber. A review of image reconstruction techniques for electrical impedance tomography. *Med. Phys.*, 16(2):162–169, 1989.

[13] D. C. Barber and B. H. Brown. Applied potential tomography. *J. Phys. E: Sci. Instrum.*, 17(9):723–733, 1984.

[14] T. Becher, T. Meinel, D. Bläser, G. Zick, N. Weiler, and I. Frerichs. Assessment of tidal recruitment and overdistension by regional analysis of respiratory system compliance at different tidal volumes. In *Proc. Int. Conf. Biomed. Appl. EIT*, volume 15, page 71, 2014.

[15] J. M. Bland and D. G. Altman. Statistical Methods for Assessing Agreement between two methods of Clinical Measurement. *The Lancet*, 327(8476):307–310, 1986.

[16] M. Bodenstein, M. David, and K. Markstaller. Principles of electrical impedance tomography and its clinical application. *Crit. Care Med.*, 37(2):713–724, 2009.

[17] S. H. Böhm. Watch the lungs breathe! EIT real-time monitoring. Technical report, Swisstom, 2013.

[18] J. B. Borges, F. Suarez-Sipmann, S. H. Böhm, G. Tusman, A. Melo, E. Maripuu, M. Sandström, M. Park, E. L. V. Costa, G. Hedenstierna, and M. Amato. Regional lung perfusion estimated by electrical impedance tomography in a piglet model of lung collapse. *J. Appl. Physiol.*, 112:225–236, 2012.

[19] S. Born, D. Iwamaru, M. Pfeifle, and D. Bartz. Three-Step Segmentation of the Lower Airways with Advanced Leakage-Control. In *The Second International Workshop On Pulmonary Image Analysis (poster)*, 2009.

[20] A. Borsic, C. McLeod, W. R. B. Lionheart, and N. Kerrouche. Realistic 2D human thorax modelling for EIT. *Physiol. Meas.*, 22:77–83, 2001.

[21] A. Boyle and A. Adler. The impact of electrode area, contact impedance and boundary shape on EIT images. *Physiol. Meas.*, 32:745–754, 2011.

[22] A. Boyle, A. Adler, and W. R. B. Lionheart. Shape Deformation in Two-Dimensional Electrical Impedance Tomography. *IEEE Trans. Med. Imaging*, 31(12):2185–2193, 2012.

[23] F. Braun, M. Proença, M. Rapin, B. Grychtol, M. Bührer, P. Krammer, S. H. Böhm, M. Lemay, J. Solà, and J.-P. Thiran. Comparing belt positions for monitoring the descending aorta by EIT. In *Proc. Int. Conf. Biomed. Appl. EIT*, volume 15, page 76, 2014.

[24] W. R. Breckon. *Image Reconstruction in electrical impedance tomography*. PhD thesis, The University of Manchester, 1990.

[25] Brown, B. H. Electrical impedance tomography (EIT): a review. *J. Med. Eng. & Tech.*, 27(3):97–108, 2003.

[26] S. Bruckner and M. E. Gröller. Style Transfer Functions for Illustrative Volume Rendering. *Computer Graphics Forum*, 26(3):715–724, 2007.

[27] S. Bruckner, M. E. Gröller, K. Mueller, B. Preim, and D. Silver. Illustrative Focus+Context Approaches in Interactive Volume Visualization. In H. Hagen, editor, *Scientific Visualization: Advanced Concepts*, Dagstuhl Follow-Ups, chapter 10. 2010.

[28] B. M. Burton, J. D. Tate, B. Erem, D. J. Swenson, D. F. Wang, M. Steffen, D. H. Brooks, P. M. van Dam, and R. S. MacLeod. A Toolkit for Forward / Inverse Problems in Electrocardiography within the SCIRun Problem Solving Environment. In *Proc. Conf. IEEE Eng. Med. Biol. Soc.*, volume 2011, pages 267–270, 2011.

[29] E. D. L. B. Camargo, F. S. Moura, O. L. Luppi, F. P. R. Martins, R. G. Lima, M. B. P. Amato, and A. C. B. C. F. Pinto. Converting CT scan images into impeditivity measurements to form an anatomical atlas for Electrical Impedance Tomography. In *Proc. Int. Congress Mechan. Eng.*, volume 21, 2011.

[30] M.-Y. Chan, Y. Wu, W.-H. Mak, W. Chen, and H. Qu. Perception-based Transparency Optimization for Direct Volume Rendering. *IEEE Trans. Vis. & Comput. Graphics (TVCG)*, 15(6):1283–1290, 2009.

[31] T. F. Chan and L. A. Vese. Active Contours Without Edges. *IEEE Trans. Image Proc.*, 10(2):266–277, 2001.

[32] Y. Chen, Y. Li, H. Guo, Y. Hu, L. Luo, X. Yin, J. Gu, and C. Toumoulin. CT Metal Artifact Reduction Method Based on Improved Image Segmentation and Sinogram In-Painting. *Math. Problems in Eng.*, 2012:786281, 2012.

[33] M. Cheney, D. Isaacson, J. C. Newell, S. Simske, and J. Goble. NOSER: An algorithm for solving the inverse conductivity problem. *Int. J. Imaging Systems & Tech.*, 2(2):66–75, 1990.

[34] D. R. Chittajallu, P. Balanca, and I. A. Kakadiaris. Automatic delineation of the inner thoracic region in non-contrast CT data. In *Proc. Conf. IEEE Eng. Med. Biol. Soc.*, volume 2009, pages 3569–3572, 2009.

[35] A. P. Condurache, E. A. Essah, A. W. Reske, M. Seiwerts, H. Busse, T. Aach, and U. G. Hofmann. Robust rib cage segmentation in CT image series using active contour models. In *Proc. BMT-2005*, pages 421–422, Nürnberg, Germany, September 14–16 2005. VDE.

[36] E. L. V. Costa, J. B. Borges, A. Melo, F. Suarez-Sipmann, C. Toufen Jr., S. H. Böhm, and M. B. P. Amato. Bedside estimation of recruitable alveolar collapse and hyperdistension by electrical impedance tomography. *Int. Care Med.*, 35:1132–1137, 2009.

[37] E. L. V. Costa, C. N. Chaves, S. Gomes, M. A. Beraldo, M. S. Volpe, M. R. Tucci, I. A. L. Schettino, S. H. Böhm, C. R. R. Carvalho, H. Tanaka, R. G. Lima, and M. B. P. Amato. Real-time detection of pneumothorax using electrical impedance tomography. *Crit. Care Med.*, 36(4):1230–1238, 2008.

[38] M. G. Crabb, J. L. Davidson, R. Little, P. Wright, A. R. Morgan, C. A. Miller, J. H. Naish, G. J. M. Parker, R. Kikinis, H. McCann, and W. R. B. Lionheart. Mutual information as a measure of image quality for 3D dynamic lung imaging with EIT. *Physiol. Meas.*, 35:863–879, 2014.

[39] A. Criminisi, P. Pérez, and K. Toyama. Region Filling and Object Removal by Exemplar-Based Image Inpainting. *IEEE Trans. Image Proc.*, 13(9):1–13, 2004.

[40] B. Csébfalvi, B. Tóth, S. Bruckner, and M. E. Gröller. Illumination-Driven Opacity Modulation for Expressive Volume Rendering. In *Proc. of Vision, Modeling & Visualization 2012*, pages 103–109, Nov. 2012.

[41] M. Czaplik, I. Biener, A. Follmann, R. Rossaint, and S. Leonhart. Optimizing PEEP in ARDS: comparison of diverse EIT parameters. In *Proc. Int. Conf. Biomed. Appl. EIT*, volume 15, page 74, 2014.

[42] M. Dannhauer, D. Brooks, D. Tucker, and R. S. MacLeod. A pipeline for the Simulation of Transcranial Direct Current Stimulation for Realistic Human Head Models using SCIRun / BioMesh3D. In *Proc. Conf. IEEE Eng. Med. Biol. Soc.*, volume 2012, pages 5486–5489, 2012.

[43] C. de Césare, M.-J. Rendas, A.-G. Allais, and M. Perrier. Low overlap image registration based on both entropy and mutual information measures. In *OCEANS 2008*, pages 1–9, 2008.

[44] J. M. Deibele, H. Luepschen, and S. Leonhardt. Dynamic separation of pulmonary and cardiac changes in electrical impedance tomography. *Physiol. Meas.*, 29:S1–S14, 2008.

[45] M. A. Denaï, M. Mahfouf, S. Mohamad-Samuri, G. Panoutsos, B. H. Brown, and G. H. Mills. Absolute Electrical Impedance Tomography (aEIT) Guided Ventilation Therapy in Critical Care Patients: Simulations and Future Trends. *IEEE Trans. Inform. Techn. Biomed.*, 14(3):641–649, 2010.

[46] S. Diepenbrock and T. Ropinski. From Imprecise User Input to Precise Vessel Segmentations. In *Proc. EG Workshop Vis. Comput. Biol. & Med. (VCBM'12)*, pages 65–72, 2012.

[47] J. Diepstraten, D. Weiskopf, and T. Ertl. Interactive Cutaway Illustrations. In *Computer Graphics Forum*, pages 523–532, 2003.

[48] M. B. Dillencourt, H. Samet, and M. Tamminen. A General Approach to Connected-component Labeling for Arbitrary Image Representations. *J. ACM*, 39(2):253–280, Apr. 1992.

[49] F. Ding, W. K. Lewo, and S. Venkatesh. Removal of Abdominal Wall for 3D Visualization and Segmentation of Organs in CT Volume. In *Proc. IEEE Int. Conf. Image Proc.*, volume 16, pages 3377–3380, 2009.

[50] A. El-Baz, F. Khalifa, E. A., M. Nitzken, A. Soliman, P. McClure, M. A. El-Ghar, and G. Gimel'farb. A Novel Approach for Global Lung Registration Using 3D Markov-Gibbs Appearance Model. *Med. Image. Comput. Comput. Assist. Interv.*, 15(2):114–121, 2012.

[51] G. Elke, M. K. Fuld, A. F. Halaweish, B. Grychtol, N. Weiler, E. A. Hoffman, and I. Frerichs. Quantification of ventilation distribution in regional lung injury by electrical impedance tomography and xenon computed tomography. *Physiol. Meas.*, 34:1303–1318, 2013.

[52] C. Ewertsen. Image fusion between ultrasonography and CT, MRI or PET/CT for image guidance and intervention - a theoretical and clinical study. *Dan. Med. Bull.*, 57(9):B4172, 2010.

[53] T. J. Faes, H. A. van der Meij, J. C. de Munck, and R. M. Heethaar. The electric resistivity of human tissues (100 Hz - 10 MHz): A meta-analysis of review studies. *Physiol. Meas.*, 20:R1–R10, 1999.

[54] A. Fagerberg, O. Stenqvist, and A. Åneman. Electrical impedance tomography applied to assess matching of pulmonary ventilation and perfusion in a porcine experimental model. *Crit. Care*, 13:R34, 2009.

[55] W. R. Fan and H. X. Wang. 3d modelling of the human thorax for ventilation distribution measured through electrical impedance tomography. *Meas. Science and Technol.*, 21(11):115801, 2010.

[56] A. Fedorov, R. Beichel, J. Kalpathy-Cramer, J. Finet, J.-C. Fillion-Robin, S. Pujol, C. Bauer, D. Jennings, F. Fennessy, M. Sonka, J. Buatti, S. Aylward, J. Miller, S. Pieper, and R. Kikinis. 3D Slicer as an Image Computing Platform for the Quantitative Imaging Network. *Magnetic Resonance Imaging*, 30(9):1323–1341, 11 2012.

[57] D. Ferrario, B. Grychtol, A. Adler, J. Solà, S. H. Böhm, and M. Bodenstein. Toward Morphological Thoracic EIT: Major Signal Sources Correspond to Respective Organ Locations in CT. *IEEE Trans. Biomed. Eng.*, 59(11):3000–3008, 2012.

[58] I. Frerichs. Electrical impedance tomography (EIT) in applications related to lung and ventilation: a review of experimental and clinical activities. *Physiol. Meas.*, 21:R1–R21, 2000.

[59] I. Frerichs. Recent Advances in thoracic imaging by electrical impedance tomography. In *Proc. Int. Conf. Biomed. Appl. EIT*, volume 15, page 50, 2014.

[60] I. Frerichs, P. A. Dargaville, and P. C. Rimensberger. Regional respiratory inflation and deflation pressure-volume curves determined by electrical impedance tomography. *Physiol. Meas.*, 34:567–577, 2013.

[61] I. Frerichs, S. Pulletz, G. Elke, F. Reifferscheid, D. Schadler, J. Scholz, and N. Weiler. Assessment of changes in distribution of lung perfusion by electrical impedance tomography. *Respiration*, 77(3):282–291, 2009.

[62] M. K. Fuld, R. B. Easley, O. I. Saba, D. Chon, J. M. Reinhardt, E. A. Hoffman, and B. A. Simon. CT-measured regional specific volume change reflects regional ventilation in supine sheep. *J. Appl. Physiol.*, 104:1177–1184, 2008.

[63] P. Gaggero, A. Adler, and B. Grychtol. Using real data to train GREIT improves image quality. In *Proc. Int. Conf. Biomed. Appl. EIT*, volume 15, page 39, 2014.

[64] M. Gargouri, J. Tierny, E. Jolivet, P. Petit, and E. D. Angelini. Acurate and Robust Shape Descriptors for the Identification of Rib Cage Structures in CT-Images with Random Forests. In *Proc. IEEE Int. Symp. Biomed. Imaging*, volume 10, pages 65–68, 2013.

[65] C. Gillmann. Interactive Volume Visualization of Computer Tomography Data with planar Electrical Impedance Tomography Data. Bachelor thesis, University of Kaiserslautern, 2012.

[66] C. Gillmann and P. Salz. Improving Visual Communication for EIT-based Lung Research. In *IEEE Pacific Vis. Symp. (Vis. Notes)*, pages 291–295, 2014.

[67] C. Gómez-Laberge, J. H. Arnold, and G. K. Wolf. A Unified Approach for EIT Imaging of Regional Overdistension and Atelectasis in Acute Lung Injury. *IEEE Trans. Med. Imaging*, 31(3):834–842, 2012.

[68] C. Gómez-Laberge, M. J. Hogan, G. Elke, N. Weiler, I. Frerichs, and A. Adler. Data-driven classification of ventilated lung tissues using electrical impedance tomography. *Physiol. Meas.*, 32(7):903–915, 2011.

[69] L. Grady. Random Walks for Image Segmentation. *IEEE Trans. Pattern Analysis & Machine Intel.*, 28(11):1–17, 2006.

[70] B. Grychtol and A. Adler. Asymmetries in Electrical Impedance Tomography Lung Images. In *Proc. Int. Conf. Biomed. Appl. EIT*, volume 13, pages 1–4, 2012.

[71] B. Grychtol and A. Adler. Finite element meshes with electrode refinement in EIDORS. In *Proc. Int. Conf. Biomed. Appl. EIT*, volume 14, 2013.

[72] B. Grychtol and A. Adler. Uniform background assumption produces misleading lung EIT images. *Physiol. Meas.*, 34:579–593, 2013.

[73] B. Grychtol, W. R. B. Lionheart, M. Bodenstein, G. K. Wolf, and A. Adler. Impact of Model Shape Mismatch on Reconstruction Quality in Electrical Impedance Tomography. *IEEE Trans. Med. Imaging*, 31(9):1754–1760, 2012.

[74] B. Grychtol, W. R. B. Lionheart, G. K. Wolf, M. Bodenstein, and A. Adler. The importance of shape: thorax models for GREIT. In *Proc. Int. Conf. EIT, Bath, UK*, 2011.

[75] B. Grychtol, G. K. Wolf, A. Adler, and J. H. Arnold. Towards lung EIT image segmentation: automatic classification of lung tissue state from analysis of EIT monitored recruitment manoeuvres. *Physiol. Meas.*, 31:S31–S43, 2010.

[76] B. Grychtol, G. K. Wolf, and J. H. Arnold. Differences in regional pulmonary pressure-impedance curves before and after lung injury assesses with a novel algorithm. *Physiol. Meas.*, 30:S137–S148, 2009.

[77] B. Haas, T. Coradi, M. Scholz, P. Kunz, M. Huber, U. Oppitz, L. André, V. Lengkeek, D. Huyskens, A. van Esch, and R. Reddick. Automatic segmentation of thoracic and pelvic CT images for radiotherapy planning using implicit anatomic knowledge and organ-specific segmentation strategies. *Phys. Med. & Biol.*, 53(6):1751, 2008.

[78] M. Hadwiger, C. Berger, and H. Hauser. High-Quality Two-Level Volume Rendering of Segmented Data Sets on Consumer Graphics Hardware. In *Proc. 14th IEEE Vis. 2003*, VIS '03, page 40, Washington, DC, USA, 2003. IEEE Computer Society.

[79] G. Hahn, A. Just, J. Dittmar, K. H. Fromm, and M. Quintel. Synchronous absolute EIT in three thoracic planes at different gravity levels. *J. Phys.: Conf. Series*, 434(1):012039, 2013.

[80] Y. Häme, E. D. Angelini, E. A. Hoffman, R. G. Barr, and A. F. Laine. Robust Quantification of Pulmonary Emphysema with a Hidden Markov Measure Field Model. In *Proc. Int. Symp. Biomed. Imaging (ISBI)*, volume 10, pages 382–385, 2013.

[81] M. Hanke-Burgeois. *Mathematische Grundlagen der Impedanztomographie*. Johannes Gutenberg-Universität, 2004.

[82] M. S. Hassouna and A. A. Faraq. Multi-stencils fast marching methods: a highly accurate solution to the eikonal equation on cartesian domains. *IEEE Trans. Pattern. Anal. Mach. Intell.*, 29(9):1563–1574, 2007.

[83] R. P. Henderson and J. G. Webster. An Impedance Camera for Spatially Specific Measurements of the Thorax. *IEEE Trans. Biomed. Eng.*, 25(3):250–254, 1978.

[84] D. Holder, editor. *Electrical Impedance Tomography: Methods, History and Applications*. Series in Medical Physics and Biomedical Engineering, 2004.

[85] A. C. Horwood, S. J. Hogan, P. R. Goddard, and J. Rossiter. Image Normalization, a Basic Requirement for Computer-based Automatic Diagnostic Applications. Technical report, DePaul University College of Computing and Digital Media, 2001.

[86] P. Hua, Q. Song, M. Sonka, E. A. Hoffman, and J. M. Reinhardt. Segmentation of Pathological and Diseased Lung Tissue in CT Images using a Graph-Search Algorithm. In *IEEE Int. Symp. Biomed. Imaging*, pages 2072–2075, 2011.

[87] J. Hyttinen, P. Kauppinen, T. Kööbi, and J. Malmivuo. Importance of the tissue conductivity values in modelling the thorax as a volume conductor. In *Proc. Int. Conf. EMBS*, volume 19, pages 2082–2085, 1997.

[88] A. Karimov, G. Mistelbauer, J. Schmidt, P. Mindek, E. Schmidt, T. Sharipov, S. Bruckner, and E. Gröller. ViviSection: Skeleton-based Volume Editing. *Computer Graphics Forum*, 32(3):461–470, June 2013.

[89] M. Kass, A. Witkin, and D. Terzopoulos. Snakes: Active Contour Models. *Int. J. Computer Vision*, 1988:321–331, 1988.

[90] H. S. Kim, H.-S. Yoon, K. N. Trung, and G. S. Lee. Automatic Lung Segmentation in CT Images using Anisotropic Diffusion and Morphology Operation. In *Proc. IEEE Int. Conf. Comput. & Inf. Techn.*, volume 7, pages 557–561, 2007.

[91] J. Kim, S. Eberl, and D. Feng. Visualizing Dual-Modality Rendered Volumes Using a Dual-Lookup Table Transfer Function. *Computing in Science and Eng.*, 9(1):20–25, Jan. 2007.

[92] M. Kim, G. Chen, and C. Hansen. Dynamic Particle System for Mesh Extraction on the GPU. In *Proc. 5th Ann. Workshop GPGPU*, GPGPU-5, pages 38–46, New York, NY, USA, 2012. ACM.

[93] Y. Kim, J. G. Webster, and W. Tompkins. Electrical Impedance imaging of the thorax. *J. Microw. Power.*, 18(3):245–57, 1983.

[94] G. Kindlmann, R. Whitaker, T. Tasdizen, and T. Möller. Curvature-Based Transfer Functions for Direct Volume Rendering: Methods and Applications. In *Proc. 14th IEEE Visualization 2003*, VIS '03, page 67, Washington, DC, USA, 2003. IEEE Computer Society.

[95] J. Kniss, G. Kindlmann, and C. Hansen. Multidimensional Transfer Functions for Interactive Volume Rendering. *IEEE Trans. Vis. & Comput. Graphics*, 8(3):270–285, July 2002.

[96] T. T. J. P. Kockelkorn, E. M. van Rikxoort, J. C. Grutters, and B. van Ginneken. Interactive Lung Segmentation in CT Scans with Severe Abnormalities. In *Proc. IEEE Int. Conf. Biomed Imaging*, ISBI'10, pages 564–567, Piscataway, NJ, USA, 2010. IEEE Press.

[97] S. Leonhardt. Progress in Perfusion Imaging with EIT. In *Proc. Int. Conf. Biomed. Appl. EIT*, volume 15, page 51, 2014.

[98] S. Leonhardt and B. Lachmann. Electrical Impedance Tomography: The Holy Grail of ventilation and perfusion imaging? *Intensive Care Med*, 38(12):1917–1929, 2012.

[99] K. Li, X. Wu, D. Chen, and M. Sonka. Optimal Surface Segmentation in Volumetric Images - A Graph-Theoretic Approach. *IEEE Trans. Pattern Analysis & Machine Intel.*, 28(1):119–134, 2006.

[100] W. R. B. Lionheart. EIT reconstruction algorithms: pitfalls, challenges and recent developments. *Physiol. Meas.*, 25:125–142, 2004.

[101] C. Liu, J. Ma, and G. Ye. Medical Image Segmentation by Geodesic Active Contour Incorporating Region Statistical Information. In *Proc. 4th Int. Conf. Fuzzy Systems & Knowledge Discovery*, volume 3 of *FSKD '07*, pages 63–67, Washington, DC, USA, 2007. IEEE Computer Society.

[102] B. C. Lucas, M. Kazhdan, and R. H. Taylor. Multi-Object Geodesic Active Contours (MOGAC). *Med. Image. Comput. Comput. Assist. Interv.*, 15(2):404–412, 2012.

[103] S. Maisch, S. H. Böhm, J. Solà, M. S. Goepfert, J. C. Kubitz, H. P. Richter, J. Ridder, A. E. Goetz, and D. A. Reuter. Heart-lung interactions measured by electrical impedance tomography. *Crit. Care Med.*, 39(9):2173–2176, 2011.

[104] L. M. Malbouisoon, F. Préteux, L. Puybasset, P. Grenier, P. Coriat, and J.-J. Rouby. Validation of a software designed for computed tomographic (CT) measurement of lung water. *Intensive Care Med.*, 27:602–608, 2001.

[105] D. Maleike, M. Nolden, H.-P. Meinzer, and I. Wolf. Interactive segmentation framework of the Medical Imaging Interaction Toolkit. *Comput. Methods Programs Biomed.*, 96(1):72–83, 2009.

[106] Y. Mamatjan, B. Grychtol, P. Gaggero, J. Justiz, V. M. Koch, and A. Adler. Evaluation and Real-Time Monitoring of Data Quality in Electrical Impedance Tomography. *IEEE Trans. Med. Imaging*, 32(11):1997–2005, 2013.

[107] K. S. McDowell, F. Vadakkumpadan, R. Blake, J. Blauer, G. Plank, R. S. MacLeod, and N. A. Trayanova. Methodology for patient-specific modeling of atrial fibrosis as a substrate for atrial fibrillation. *J. Electrocardiol.*, 45(6):640–645, 2012.

[108] P. Metherall, R. H. Smallwood, and D. C. Barber. Three Dimensional Electrical Impedance Tomography of the Human Thorax. In *Proc. Int. Conf. IEEE Eng. in Med. & Biol. Society*, volume 18, pages 758–759, 1996.

[109] O. Moerer, G. Hahn, and M. Quintel. Lung impedance measurements to monitor alveolar ventilation. *Curr. Opin. Crit. Care*, 17(3):260–267, 2011.

[110] E. N. Mortensen and W. A. Barrett. Interactive Segmentation with Intelligent Scissors. *Graph. Models Image Process.*, 60(5):349–384, Sept. 1998.

[111] T. Muders, H. Luepschen, J. Zinserling, S. Greschus, R. Fimmers, U. Guenther, M. Buchwald, D. Grigutsch, S. Leonhardt, C. Putensen, and H. Wrigge. Tidal recruitment assessed by electrical impedance tomography and computed tomography in a porcine model of lung injury. *Crit. Care Med.*, 40(3):1–9, 2011.

[112] R. Muzzolini, Y.-H. Yang, and R. Pierson. Texture characterization using robust statistics. *Pattern Recog.*, 27(1):119–134, 1994.

[113] S. Nebuya, T. Koike, H. Imai, I. Y., N. Khambete, H. Kumagai, K. Soma, and B. H. Brown. Comparison between regional lung CT values and lung densities estimated using EIT. In *Proc. Int. Conf. Biomed. Appl. EIT*, volume 15, page 70, 2014.

[114] A. Nissinen, V. Kolehmainen, and J. P. Kaipio. Compensation of errors due to incorrect model geometry in electrical impedance tomography. *J. Phys.: Conf. Series*, 224:012050, 2010.

[115] M. Nolden, S. Zelzer, A. Seitel, D. Wald, M. Müller, A. M. Franz, D. Maleike, M. Fangerau, M. Baumhauer, L. Maier-Hein, K. H. Maier-Hein, H.-P. Meinzer, and I. Wolf. The Medical Imaging Interaction Toolkit: challenges and advances. *Int. J. CARS*, 8:607–620, 2013.

[116] P. Perona and J. Malik. Scale-Space and Edge Detection Using Anisotropic Diffusion. *IEEE Trans. Pattern Analysis Machine Intel.*, 12(7):629–639, 1990.

[117] R. Pikkemaat and S. Leonhardt. Separation of ventilation and perfusion related signals within EIT-data streams. *J. Phys.: Conf. Series*, 224:012028, 2010.

[118] C. Preis, H. Luepschen, S. Leonhardt, and D. Gommers. Experimental case report: development of a pneumothorax monitored by electrical impedance tomography. *Clin. Physiol. Funct. Imaging*, 29(3):159–162, 2009.

[119] M. Proença, F. Braun, M. Rapin, J. Solà, A. Adler, B. Grychtol, M. Bührer, P. Krammer, S. H. Böhm, M. Lemay, and J.-P. Thiran. Influence of heart motion on EIT-based stroke volume estimation. In *Proc. Int. Conf. Biomed. Appl. EIT*, volume 15, page 77, 2014.

[120] J. Pu, J. Roos, C. A. Yi, S. Napel, G. D. Rubin, and D. S. Paik. Adaptive border marching algorithm: Automatic lung segmentation on chest {CT} images. *Comput. Med. Imaging & Graphics*, 32(6):452–462, 2008.

[121] S. Pulletz, A. Adler, M. Kott, G. Elke, B. Gawelczyk, D. Schädler, G. Zick, N. Weiler, and I. Frerichs. Regional lung opening and closing pressures in patients with acute lung injury. *J. Crit. Care.*, 27(3):323, 2012.

[122] S. Pulletz, H. R. van Genderingen, G. Schmitz, G. Zick, S. D., J. Scholz, N. Weiler, and I. Frerichs. Comparison of different methods to define regions of interest for evaluation of regional lung ventilation by EIT. *Physiol. Meas.*, 27(5):S115–S127, 2006.

[123] C. Putensen, H. Wrigge, and J. Zinserling. Electrical Impedance tomography guided ventilation therapy. *Curr. Opin. Crit. Care*, 13:344–350, 2007.

[124] S. Raghunath, S. Rajagopalan, R. A. Karwoski, M. R. Bruesewitz, C. H. McCollough, B. J. Bartholmai, and R. A. Robb. Landscaping the Effect of CT Reconstruction Parameters: Robust Interstitial Pulmonary Fibrosis Quantitation. In *Proc. Int. Symp. Biomed. Imaging (ISBI)*, volume 10, pages 374–377, 2013.

[125] T. Rahman, M. M. Hasan, A. Farooq, and M. Z. Uddin. Extraction of cardiac and respiration signals in electrical impedance tomography based on independent component analysis. *J. Electr. Bioimp.*, 4:38–44, 2013.

[126] P. Rautek, S. Bruckner, and E. Gröller. Semantic Layers for Illustrative Volume Rendering. *IEEE Trans. Vis. & Comput. Graphics (TVCG)*, 13(6):1336–1343, Nov. 2007.

[127] F. Reifferscheid, G. Elke, S. Pulletz, B. Gawelczyk, I. Lautenschläger, M. Steinfath, N. Weiler, and I. Frerichs. Regional ventilation distribution determined by electrical impedance tomography: Reproducability and effects of posture and chest plane. *Respirology*, 16:523–531, 2011.

[128] A. W. Reske, H. Busse, M. B. P. Amato, M. Jaekel, T. Kahn, P. Schwarzkopf, D. Schreiter, U. Gottschaldt, and M. Seiwerts. Image Reconstruction affects computer tomographic assessment of lung hyperinflation. *Intensive Care Med.*, 34:2044–2053, 2008.

[129] A. W. Reske, A. Rau, A. P. Reske, M. Koziol, B. Gottwald, M. Alef, J.-C. Ionita, P. M. Spieth, P. Hepp, M. Seiwerts, A. Beda, S. Born, G. Scheuermann, M. B. P. Amato, and H. Wrigge. Extrapolation in the analysis of lung aeration by computed tomography: a validation study. *Critical Care*, 15:R279, 2011.

[130] A. W. Reske, A. P. Reske, H. A. Gast, M. Seiwerts, A. Beda, U. Gottschaldt, C. Josten, D. Schreiter, N. Heller, H. Wrigge, and M. B. Amato. Extrapolation from ten section can make CT-based quantification of lung aeration more practicable. *Intensive Care Med.*, 36:1836–1844, 2010.

[131] A. W. Reske, A. P. Reske, T. Heine, P. M. Spieth, A. Rau, M. Seiwerts, H. Busse, U. Gottschaldt, D. Schreiter, S. Born, M. Gama de Abreu, C. Josten, H. Wrigge, and M. B. P. Amato. Computed tomographic assessment of lung weights in trauma patients with early posttraumatic lung dysfunction. *Critical Care*, 15:R71, 2011.

[132] T. Ropinski and K. H. Hinrichs, editors. *Real-Time Rendering of 3D Magic Lenses having arbitrary convex Shapes*, Proc. 12th Int. Conf. Comput. Graphics, Vis. & Comput., WWU Münster, 2004.

[133] D. Rueckert, P. Burger, S. M. Forbat, R. D. Mohiaddin, and G. Z. Yang. Automatic Tracking of the Aorta in Cardiovascular MR Images Using Deformable Models. *IEEE Trans. Med. Imaging*, 16(5):581–590, 1997.

[134] P. Salz and G. Reis. Time-dynamic Volume Visualization of Multimodally Tagged Body Cells. In *Proc. 8th IASTED Int. Conf. Vis. Imaging & Image Proc.*, pages 137–142. ACTA Press, 2008.

[135] P. Salz, G. Reis, and D. Stricker. Texture-based Tracking in mm-wave Images. In C. Garth, A. Middel, and H. Hagen, editors, *Visualization of Large and Unstructured Data Sets: Applications in Geospatial Planning, Modeling and Engineering - Proceedings of IRTG 1131 Workshop 2011*, volume 27 of *OpenAccess Series in Informatics (OASIcs)*, pages 89–101, Dagstuhl, Germany, 2012. Schloss Dagstuhl–Leibniz-Zentrum fuer Informatik.

[136] P. Salz, A. W. Reske, H. Wrigge, G. Scheuermann, and H. Hagen. An Interactive Workflow to segment Thoracic CT Data for Electrical Impedance Tomography Image Reconstruction. In *EG Workshop Vis. Comp. Biol. & Med. (Poster)*, 2012.

[137] P. Salz, A. W. Reske, H. Wrigge, G. Scheuermann, and H. Hagen. User-guided Segmentation of Thoracic Computed Tomography Data for Electrical Impedance Tomography Image Reconstruction. In *IEEE Int. Conf. Biol. Data Vis. (Poster)*, 2012.

[138] P. Salz, A. W. Reske, H. Wrigge, G. Scheuermann, and H. Hagen. Improving Electrical Impedance Tomography Imaging of the Lung with Patient-specific 3D Models. In *Visualization in Medicine and Life Sciences*, pages 49–53. The Eurographics Association, 2013.

[139] P. Salz, A. W. Reske, H. Wrigge, G. Scheuermann, and H. Hagen. Towards patient-specific Electrical Impedance Tomography: A precise

anatomical model for image reconstruction. In *Proc. Int. Conf. Biomed. Appl. EIT (Abstract)*, volume 14, 2013.

[140] J. A. Schmidt, C. R. Johnson, J. C. Eason, and R. S. MacLeod. Applications of Automatic Mesh Generation and Adaptive Methods in Computational Medicine. In I. Babuska, J. Flaherty, W. Henshaw, J. Hopcroft, J. Oliger, and T. Tezduyar, editors, *Modeling, Mesh Generation, and Adaptive Methods for Partial Differential Equations*, pages 367–390. Springer-Verlag, 1995.

[141] T. Shen, H. Li, and X. Huang. Active Volume Models for Medical Image Segmentation. *IEEE Trans. Med. Imaging*, 30(3):774–791, 2011.

[142] P. Sikachev, P. Rautek, S. Bruckner, and M. E. Gröller. Dynamic Focus+Context for Volume Rendering. In *Proc. of Vision, Modeling & Visualization 2010*, pages 331–338, University of Siegen, Siegen, Germany, Nov. 2010.

[143] I. C. Sluimer, M. Niemeijer, and B. van Ginneken. Lung field segmentation from thin-slice CT scans in presence of severe pathology. In *Proc. SPIE*, volume 5370, pages 1447–1455, 2004.

[144] M. Sofka, J. Wetzl, N. Birkbeck, J. Zhang, T. Kohlberger, J. Kaftan, J. Declerck, and S. K. Zhou. Multi-stage Learning for Robust Lung Segmentation in Challenging CT Volumes. *Med. Image Comput. Comput. Assist. Interv.*, 14(3):667–674, 2011.

[145] J. Solà, A. Adler, A. Santos, G. Tusman, F. S. Sipmann, and S. H. Böhm. Non-invasive monitoring of central blood pressure by electrical impedance tomography: first experimental evidence. *Med. Biol. Eng. Comput.*, 49:409–415, 2011.

[146] J. Solà, R. Vetter, P. Renevey, O. Chételat, C. Sartori, and S. F. Rimoldi. Parametric estimation of pulse arrival time: a robust approach to pulse wave velocity. *Physiol. Meas.*, 30:603–615, 2009.

[147] M. Soleimani, C. Gómez-Laberge, and A. Adler. Imaging of conductivity changes and electrode movement in EIT. *Physiol. Meas.*, 27:S103–S113, 2006.

[148] V. Soltészovà, L. E. S. Helljesen, W. Wein, O. H. Gilja, and I. Viola. Lowest-Variance Streamlines for Filtering of 3D Ultrasound. In *EG Workshop Vis. Comp. Biol. & Med.*, pages 41–48, 2012.

[149] E. Somersalo, M. Cheney, and D. Isaacson. Existence and Uniqueness for Electrode Models for Electric Current Computed Tomography. *SIAM J. Appl. Math.*, 52(4):1023–1040, 1992.

[150] S. Sun, C. Bauer, and R. Beicel. Automated 3-D Segmentation of Lungs With Lung Cancer in CT Data Using a Novel Robust Active Shape Model Approach. *IEEE Trans. Med. Imaging*, 31(2):449–460, 2012.

[151] G. Székely, A. Kelemen, C. Brechbühler, and G. Gerig. Segmentation of 2-D and 3-D objects from MRI volume data using constrained elastic deformations of flexible Fourier contour and surface models. *Med. Image. Analysis*, 1(1):19–34, 1996.

[152] E. Teschner and M. Imhoff. Electrical Impedance Tomography: The realization of regional ventilation monitoring. Technical report, Dräger, 2011.

[153] A. Tizzard, A. Borsic, R. Halter, and R. Bayford. Generation and performance of patient-specific forward models for breast imaging with EIT. *J. Phys.: Conf. Series*, 224:012034, 2010.

[154] A. Tizzard, J. M. Khor, A. Demosthenous, and R. Bayford. Wearable sensors for patient-specific boundary shape estimation. In *Proc. Int. Conf. Biomed. Appl. EIT*, volume 15, page 7, 2014.

[155] C. Tomas and R. Manduchi. Bilateral Filtering for Gray and Color Images. In *Proc. 6th Int. Conf. Comput. Vision*, pages 839–846, 1998.

[156] A. Top, G. Hamarneh, and R. Abugharbieh. Active Learning for Interactive 3D Image Segmentation. In *Proc. 14th Int. Conf. Med. Image Comput. & Comput. Assist. Interv.*, volume 3 of *MICCAI'11*, pages 603–610, Berlin, Heidelberg, 2011. Springer-Verlag.

[157] R. Unnikrishnan and M. Hebert. Measures of Similarity. In *IEEE Workshop Appl. Comp. Vision*, volume 7, pages 394–400, 2005.

[158] R. C. Veltkamp. Shape matching: Similarity measures and algorithms. In *Proc. Int. Conf. Shape Modeling & Appl.*, SMI '01, pages 188–, Washington, DC, USA, 2001. IEEE Computer Society.

[159] Y. Wan, H. Otsuna, C.-B. Chien, and C. Hansen. Interactive extraction of neural structures with user-guided morphological diffusion. In *Proc. IEEE Int. Symp. Biol. Data Vis. (BioVis'12)*, pages 1–8, 2012.

[160] D. Wang, R. M. Kirby, R. S. MacLeod, and C. R. Johnson. Inverse Electrocardiographic Source Localization of Ischemia: An Optimization Framework and Finite Element Solution. *J. Comput. Phys.*, 250:403–424, 2013.

[161] H. Wang and P. A. Yushkevich. Guiding Automatic Segmentation with Multiple Manual Segmentations. *Med. Image. Comput. Comput. Assist. Interv.*, 15(2):429–436, 2012.

[162] L. Wang, Y. Zhao, K. Mueller, and A. Kaufman. The Magic Volume Lens: An Interactive Focus+Context Technique for Volume Rendering. In *Proc. IEEE Visualization 2005 (VIS'05)*, VIS '05, pages 367—374, 2005.

[163] J. Wei, L. Chen, G. A. Sandison, Y. Liang, and L. X. Xu. X-ray CT high-density artefacrt suppression in the presence of bones. *Phys. Med. Biol.*, 49:5407–5418, 2004.

[164] W. Wein, B. Röper, and N. Navab. Automatic Registration and Fusion of Ultrasound with CT for Radiotherapy. *Med. Image. Comput. Comput. Assist. Interv.*, 8(2):303–311, 2005.

[165] D. Weiskopf, K. Engel, and T. Ertl. Volume clipping via per-fragment operations in texture-based volume visualization. In *IEEE Visualization, 2002*, pages 93–100, 2002.

[166] J. Williams and J. Rossignac. Tightening: curvature-limiting morphological simplification. In *Proc. ACM symp. Solid & Phys. Modeling*, SPM '05, pages 107–112, New York, NY, USA, 2005. ACM.

[167] G. K. Wolf, B. Grychtol, T. K. Boyd, D. Zurakowski, and J. H. Arnold. Regional overdistension identified with electrical impedance tomography in the perflubron-treated lung. *Physiol. Meas.*, 31:S85–S95, 2010.

[168] E. J. Woo, P. Hua, J. G. Webster, and W. J. Tompkins. Finite-element method in electrical impedance tomography. *Med. & Biol. Eng. & Comput.*, 32:530–536, 1994.

[169] H. Wrigge and A. W. Reske. Patient-Ventilator Asynchrony: Adapt the Ventilator, Not the Patient! *Crit. Care Med.*, 41(9):2240–2241, 2013.

[170] H. Wrigge, J. Zinserling, T. Muders, D. Varelmann, U. Günther, C. von der Groeben, A. Magnusson, G. Hedenstierna, and C. Putensen. Electrical impedance tomography compared with thoracic computed tomography during a slow inflation maneuver in experimental models of lung injury. *Crit. Care Med.*, 36(3):903–909, 2008.

[171] R. Yalamanchili, D. Chittajallu, P. Balanca, B. Tamarappoo, D. Berman, D. Dey, and I. Kakadiaris. Automatic Segmentation of the Diaphragm in non-contrast CT Images. In *IEEE Int. Symp. Biomed. Eng.*, pages 900–903, 2010.

[172] F. Yang, J. Zhang, and R. Patterson. Development of an anatomically realistic forward solver for thoracic electrical impedance tomography. *J. Med. Eng.*, 2013:983938, 2013.

[173] W. Yang, X. Wang, L. Lin, and C. Gao. Interactive CT Image Segmentation with Online Discriminative Learning. In *Proc. IEEE Int. Conf. Image Proc.*, volume 18, pages 425–428, 2011.

[174] Y. Yim, M. Wakid, C. Kirmizibayrak, S. Bielamowicz, and J. Hahn. Registration of 3D CT Data to 2D Endoscopic Image using a Gradient Mutual Information based Viewpoint Matching for Image-Guided Medialization Laryngoplasty. *J. Comput. Science & Eng.*, 4(4):368–387, 2010.

[175] J. Zaporozhan, S. Ley, R. Eberhardt, O. Weinheimer, S. Iliyushenko, F. Herth, and H.-U. Kauczor. Paired Inspiratory / Expiratory Volumet-

ric Thin-Slice CT Scan for Emphysema Analysis. *Chest*, 128(5):3212–3220, 2005.

[176] Z. Zhao, A. Adler, K. Möller, and B. Grychtol. GREIT is sensitive to training targets near boundary. In *Proc. Int. Conf. Biomed. Appl. EIT*, volume 15, page 59, 2014.

[177] Z. Zhao, I. Frerichs, S. Pulletz, U. Müller-Lisse, and K. Möller. Does thorax EIT image analysis depend on the image reconstruction method? *J. Phys.: Conf. Series*, 434(1):012040, 2013.

[178] Z. Zhao, S. Krüger-Ziolek, B. Schullcke, and K. Möller. Lung tissue measured in EIT may change depending on the positioning of electrode plane. In *Proc. Int. Conf. Biomed. Appl. EIT*, volume 15, page 78, 2014.

I want morebooks!

Buy your books fast and straightforward online - at one of the world's fastest growing online book stores! Environmentally sound due to Print-on-Demand technologies.

Buy your books online at
www.get-morebooks.com

Kaufen Sie Ihre Bücher schnell und unkompliziert online – auf einer der am schnellsten wachsenden Buchhandelsplattformen weltweit! Dank Print-On-Demand umwelt- und ressourcenschonend produziert.

Bücher schneller online kaufen
www.morebooks.de

OmniScriptum Marketing DEU GmbH
Heinrich-Böcking-Str. 6-8
D - 66121 Saarbrücken

Telefax: +49 681 93 81 567-9

info@omniscriptum.de
www.omniscriptum.de

Printed by Books on Demand GmbH, Norderstedt / Germany